A Guide to Better eLearning

Everything you need to know to start creating effective online learning content

By Scott Cooper

Contents

Chapter 1:
Why Learning is
Important

Life is one big learning experience and it starts the second that we are born. As a newborn, we learn to breathe, eat and adapt to our new surroundings. Soon after this, we start to discover the world, and everything that we do becomes a learning experience. A few years into our lives we are exposed to our first structured learning experiences and for around the next fifteen or so years we are (ideally) a sponge, soaking up every piece of knowledge that we can absorb. Even though the first quarter of our life is the most intense in our learning and development stage, it doesn't mean that we stop learning there.

'You learn something new every day.' How many times have you heard this old saying? Learning is a part of daily life and even though some people might think that they never learn anything new, every single day they are learning new things, even if they don't realize it at the time. The world we are living in is changing at a rapid pace and the ability to learn and keep up is one of the most important skills anyone can have. A recent study has shown that learning something brings you more happiness than playing or watching sport, or gambling in a casino.

It's actually almost impossible to not learn something new every day!

Learning makes us who we are as a person. Everyone wants to learn different things and this is one of the most exciting and important things about our society. Just how boring would it be if we all only wanted to eat the same food, or wear the same clothes? Well, it would be just as boring if we all only wanted to learn the same things.

One of the most rewarding things that anyone can do is teach a person something new. 'Give a man a fish and he'll have food for a day; teach a man to fish and he'll have food for a lifetime.' The same philosophy rings true for learning. If you are always only given the answers, you will never learn to solve a problem yourself. By learning how to solve problems, you are increasing your knowledge that is then applicable to many other areas of life outside of the initial problem.

There are many misconceptions surrounding learning, based off the fact that people didn't enjoy what they were forced to learn when they were in school. They then have a negative image implanted in their head and believe that you have to be sitting in a classroom to learn anything. The average person learns hundreds of things every day. These range from little things like their bus timetable, or what to wear to keep warm during the cold weather, all the way through to new professional development skills at work, or world politics that you read online during your lunch break. Ninety-three percent of people believe that we are never too old to learn.

Another common misconception is that learning should be fast and (preferably) easy. This is not at all true. Learning takes time. Think of the phrase 'to be taught a lesson.' That invokes almost the feeling of pain. Not everyone has a photographic memory, and this is why, when you are learning a new concept (whether that be algebra or doing a profit and loss) you will spend days, if not weeks studying the same concept and working through problems. This is so that you can understand variables and learn the material a lot more thoroughly.

As far as learning being confusing, if you are not confused at some stage then you should be learning something harder! Confusion is the sweat of learning. If you think of learning like a process similar to going to the gym - when you are working out you sweat and afterwards you are sore. Similarly, when you learn, it's okay to get confused. Confusion shouldn't be something that you are scared of, it means that you are thinking about your subject and how to best understand it.

Changing the Way that We Learn

In the same way that the world is changing at a rapid pace, so too is the way that we learn. It used to be that if you wanted to read a book such as the one you are reading right now, you would need to find a local bookstore, and then wait for them to stock the title you are looking for, or order in a copy. Those days are gone, and if we can find more than two or three bookstores in our cities we are doing well. Where in the past, books were heavily relied on as a learning tool, now almost every person on the planet has their own personal learning tool in their pocket.

By the time the mid-1990s rolled around, the internet had entered households across the world and the way that we learn was starting to change forever. While there were still some doubters hanging around, the longer time went on the more people were starting to embrace sitting down at their computer to learn something new, and for many sitting at

their computer was a learning experience in itself!
However, this was only the beginning.

The internet gave us all access to anything from anywhere
in the world at any time and changed the way that we
thought. No longer were we reliant on someone to tell us
what stories would be put under our nose, we could read
and learn whatever we wanted and not be limited in
sources. This took the blinders off the public when it came
to finding out what was happening in the world and paved
the way for modern learning and journalism.

Around the time that the internet was starting to grow in
popularity with the general public, another invention was
also first released and would change the way that the world
functioned forever.

The IBM Simon might not look very impressive to us now,
but this was the original smartphone - the technology that
would have the biggest impact on how we would learn
forever. Of course, the original smartphones were not the
greatest tools at this point in time, but over the next ten
years smart phones were developed into a must-have item
for every person across the world. If you walked into a

school today, you would see almost every child with a laptop and a smartphone, replacing the books and pencils of only ten years ago.

One of the greatest things about the evolution of these technologies is that not only are we constantly improving the way that we interact with each other and how the world operates, we are also constantly learning. Every time there is a new operating system release, we are learning about all of the new features. When some exciting new software is released, we learn how to use it. Technology is constantly evolving, and whether we realize it or not, we are spending time every single day learning new things!

By why is that important? Why should we be constantly learning?

The human brain is a muscle, just like any other part of your body. And just like any other part of your body, if you don't work out your muscles they will get weak. Unlike other muscles where you might have to go to a gym or for a walk to work out, you can easily exercise your brain by reading or doing something as simple as playing a game or solving a puzzle. There are even a number of companies now that specifically focus on brain training and measuring your improvement. If you ever find that you easily forget things, this is a great way to improve your memory.

Education and Learning

We always have to remember that the ability to learn is what has got the human race to the point that we are at now. If you think back through history, the people that we remember are the people that were the greatest learners of their time.

Isaac Newton didn't just come up with the concept of gravity after an apple fell on his head; he spent his lifetime studying a range of concepts that all helped to lead him to this discovery. The same can be said for Albert Einstein, and Alexander Graham Bell. Bell made some of the greatest discoveries that changed the world, and he didn't stop after he invented one thing. His lifetime of learning led to hundreds of inventions that not only improved his life, but everyone who came after him.

That's what learning is all about - educating ourselves to understand and improve the world for everyone. If it wasn't for people like Einstein and Bell learning and discovering the concepts that they spent their lives working on, we may not have progressed as much as we have today. They have laid the groundwork for the next generation of inventors to step up and learn to improve their systems, and after them the next generation will do the same again.

We are now well and truly moving into the digital age, and modern day inventors might not all have impressive beards (although some do!), but they are all a little quirky in their own way. Bill Gates, Steve Jobs and Mark Zuckerberg are the inventors of our time and have shown us very different ways of learning compared to their predecessors, and that not everybody will respond to the same learning programs.

What do all three of these impressive leaders have in common?

None of them finished college? Yes. But they are all still highly intelligent and educated (both book smart and also business smart), and had the chance to take advantage of a great gap in the market at the time. Education is one of the cornerstones of American culture. Until recently, if you didn't have a college degree on your resume a lot of employers wouldn't even consider reading it, let alone hiring you to work for them!

All three of these men started attending college only to drop out and pursue building companies of their own which developed into Microsoft, Apple and Facebook. Obviously, all of these companies have changed the world as we have moved into the digital age, but they have also taught us that learning is not a defined thing, and there is no right or wrong way to go about learning.

Online universities are fast becoming the most popular way to get educated and still be accredited for your studies. This allows the learner to be able to learn at their own pace at a time that suits them. Rather than sitting in a classroom for set hours of the day, learning material that is targeted to the learning needs of a room full of people, instead of their individual learning needs.

Online learning allows students to get much more out of the experience because they are going to be constantly engaged in the subject matter. Not only that, it also means that anyone can enroll! Whether you are coming out of high school, are a stay-at-home parent, or have been working for many years and are looking for a career change, online universities offer the freedom to be able to learn what you want, when you want.

On-the-Job Learning

Another alternative to a traditional university has been around since ancient Greek and Egyptian times. 'On-the-job learning' is a term that has become a lot more common in recent times, but when it comes down to it apprenticeships have been around for a long time. Over thousands of years, apprenticeships have help shape the world and taught countless generations new skills that they have then been able to pass on to their own apprentices.

On-the-job learning is really just a modern take on apprenticeships as we move into the digital age, but the concept is just as important today as it was when Rome was being built. There are a number of companies around now that hire on culture and attitude rather than purely your education. But why would they be doing this?

It actually makes a lot of sense. Companies are not hiring less qualified people by any means; they are still hiring very smart people, but they also must be the right people. Having a college degree doesn't necessarily make you the right person for the job, but it's a great start.

Ideal candidates have generally come from backgrounds where they have been learning on their own, working on outside projects, and building up their skill set. Being able to do this shows a potential employer a lot about a person's character and how they are willing to work on their own to learn and develop their skills outside of the 'normal' channels.

This is also how entrepreneurs get their starts. They are not lucky because they get a big break. They have put many years of hard work and learning into what they do to become an expert. People with this mindset and background are incredibly valuable to young businesses, especially in technology. The ability to be able to think outside of the norm is a skill that needs to be developed by the individual and can't be taught in a classroom.

Building a team around culture and people who have this background, combined with technically minded people, is a great combination for success. Learning on-the-job is becoming a more common option for a lot of young people with these types of backgrounds. The job market is changing quickly, and with more of the market moving into the technology field, being able to study specifically for these positions is not always an option and learning on-the-job is a must. Because technology is now starting to advance much faster than educational institutions can keep up with, it can take three to four years before a training program can be developed around some career paths, which by then is too late.

This is why on-the-job training is so critical, and employers need to provide time for their team to learn. In saying this, that doesn't necessarily mean that everyone needs a ridged training program in their workplace, but it does mean that staff need time away from their regular duties to learn on their own.

We need to remember that when we talk about learning it is not a set thing. This could mean that one week we might be completing an eLearning course, but the next week we might be reading up on how to make the most of your time through a cool blog post that you've found online, or watching a TED Talk about how to evaluate ideas. There is no right or wrong way to learn, but the most important thing is to make time for learning!

A great way to get into a good learning routine is by blocking out time every week for learning new things and setting a different theme for each week of the month. As an example, for the first week of each month you might learn a new time management skill; the second could be improving your writing or presentation skills; the third team leadership and management; and the fourth learning a new system.

Setting a structure like this allows you to revisit those topics or ideas every month and build off what you have previously learnt. It is also a great idea for you to document what you learn in each of these sessions, so that you can then present your learning to your colleagues at the end of the month and swap stories on what worked best and what you'd recommend for others to learn.

Training our teams, or running training programs with our colleagues, has become easier than ever and is critical to running a successful business. With the help of a learning management system you can easily create customizable training programs for your team, for everything from onboarding, to how to add a new client to your system, and for training new sales team members.

What was your last training experience like? Was it fun? Was it relevant?

If you, like most people have spent your training time at work sitting in a large conference room with a large group of people running through a Powerpoint presentation that's probably at least five years old, then you need to speak to your manager about changing the way that your company looks at training.

Training shouldn't just be something that a business needs to do so that they don't get a fine from the government - it should be a fun and exciting process for everyone involved. It's great to see so many companies putting the focus on professional development programs where employees can have the chance to grow in the areas that they want to grow. This is not only great for the employee, but it's also great for the business. Employees learning new skills will only help to improve the way that they think. They will then teach other people within the organization what they have learnt which will improve the skills of everyone around them.

Just imagine if you have 50 employees, and each one of those employees has been learning a unique skill that they can then teach the other 49 team members? That's a lot of knowledge right there, and we'd be crazy to not make the most of it!

Everyone has their own way of learning. Even with all of the modern technology, it's still nice to sit back and relax with a good old--fashioned book in your hands. Everybody has the methods that work for them and that's great, but you should always play to your strengths. If you like watching videos, watch more TED Talks. If you like reading, get more awesome books. If you like learning with people, find a meetup group and get out to learn with some like-minded people.

There is no right or wrong way to learn, as long as you're learning.

Take a look at children growing up now. Their development is as important as ever, but the range of tools that they have to learn the basics of life has expanded exponentially over the past ten years! When I was young and growing up the thought of having a computer in the house was shocking to most people, whereas now it's not at all uncommon to see a child less than three years old with an iPad and actually using it to play a game or watch a video. They know where all the buttons are to make everything happen, and need little to no assistance.

If that is what is happening with children growing up now, what will children be learning in another ten years?

With the introduction of driverless cars, smart watches, Google Glass and more, we can already see that the world is going to continue to evolve at a rapid pace and the ability to learn and move with the times will be more critical than ever. I'm sure we all have a parent or relative who is still grappling with the intricacies of how to use their new smartphone. But even now there are plenty of grandparents who have embraced learning in their older age and now use email on a daily basis while speaking to their families via Skype.

This raises another important point that we can never forget - no one is ever too old to learn something new. Plenty of old dogs have been taught new tricks and we are no different.

From my own personal experience, I have found that as I have grown older, I have grown more passionate about learning and being able to teach others the skills that I have learned so they can use them too. One of the most rewarding things that we can do is teach someone how to do something new. It could be anything, but you can see the excitement in their eyes when everything starts to come together and make sense for them.

We've talked about why learning is important but what would happen if everyone decided that they didn't need to learn anything else?

This is a very scary thought, but believe it or not there are people out there who think that they don't need to learn anything new. They don't realize it, but they are actually still learning things every day. The thing is, if the people that are not wanting to learn let down their guards, they would actually take in a lot more information and discover a whole new world that would help to improve them as a person and then improve their community.

Imagine a community where everyone encouraged each other to be constantly learning new things and pushing themselves as people. This would be a great place to live and lead to a more positive culture of development and forward thinking.

Back in the 1980s there was a huge assortment of movies that were released around the rise of the 'geek' or 'nerds' and with that both of these terms have been associated with negative thoughts until the mid 2000s. Sick of being labelled as push-overs and weak, we saw a rise in the smart people of the world to reclaim both terms and encourage younger people that it's okay to be a geek or nerd. Why should it ever be 'uncool' to learn new things and help to improve the world?

This push empowered a lot of young people, known as Generation Z, who before may have been too scared to step out and show off the great things that they have learnt or created, to become the fastest learning and most accepting generation that the world has ever seen.

The more that we can learn about each other and the world we live in, the better we can make the world. Because if we can't learn from the mistakes of our parents, grandparents and ancestors, we are doomed to make the exact same mistakes all over again.

Chapter 2: The Need for Learning to Drive Innovation

By Ricardo Sé Cestari

Innovation is the word of the 21st century. We are soaked by it. We crave and fear it as individuals. Every day, we desire more of it even though we already use a variety of devices, tools and services that, just recently, deeply changed the way we live our lives. However, people also feel insecure and threatened by what they don't know. And innovation, by definition, is the realization of something that was not predicted and that considerably changed the status quo. People feel insecure because innovation makes things obsolete, and people do not want to be obsolete themselves.

At the organizational level, every company in most industries in the world today is threatened by innovation or excited and motivated by it. At most times they are both, just like individuals. We see innovation destroying the status-quo in industry after industry, from taxi (Uber) to recruiting (Seek / LinkedIn), from accommodation (AirBnB) to accounting (Xero), from entertainment (NetFlix / Spotify / YouTube) to medicine (CRISPR), from space flight (SpaceX) to filmmaking (DSLR-shot movies and desktop editing), from personal communication (smartphones) to personal relationships (Facebook / online games / dating sites) - all of it ultimately changing forever who we are and how we live.

Due to this, every organization is desperate to be innovative these days. The threat of being killed by a young disruptive startup looms at every corner. Yet, uncountable directives to be innovative coming from the top fail. Very often, large budgets are allocated to fuel innovation-related projects and little is actually accomplished. The quest to be innovative has many misconceptions and extreme challenges, and that is true for large organizations, for smaller ones and also for individuals.

Innovation requires an environment that promotes and sustains it, in both organizations and in our personal lives. Certain core values and general behaviors need to be abundant in the individual and in the environment so that innovation seeds can come into being, be planted, fertilized and can grow properly.

These vital core values for innovation include the following:

1. Diversity
2. Open and honest communication
3. Accepting and driving change
4. Selflessness and teamwork
5. Courage and acceptance of failure
6. Autonomy
7. Continuous learning

Diversity

Ideas feed and grow from each other. It is a condition of their conception and their evolution into something useful and successful. Steven Johnson, in his excellent TED Talk, put this clearly:

> "We take ideas from other people, from people we've learned from, from people we run into in the coffee shop, and we stitch them together into new forms and we create something new."

In his talk, he mentions that most of the ideas in the Enlightenment period have a coffee house in their story. In the coffee house environment, at that time, there were people from different backgrounds, different fields of expertise, openly chatting about their experiences, mistakes, successes and ideas. In that environment, there were:

> "different ideas together, different backgrounds, different interests, jostling with each other, bouncing off each other. That environment is the environment that leads to innovation."

Innovation depends on diversity, both in the workplace, where people can have contact and open communication with other people from a variety of backgrounds and expertise; and also at the personal level, where the most travelled people, with the most life experiences, with a variety of hobbies and interests and with the most curiosity to learn about things, usually are the most creative and innovative people.

Diversity enables ideas to be born; it is vital for the conception and metamorphosis of ideas into successful things.

Open and Honest Communication

As mentioned, innovation depends on open communication, especially in the workplace. As in the coffee house story, people create and morph ideas in environments where open and honest communication are present. In organizations, the more people feel they are open to honestly talk about their experiences, mistakes and challenges, the more other people will contribute with different points-of-view and possible solutions. And the richness of these points-of-views will depend on diversity.

We can often notice many organizations struggling to be innovative when there is little space for people to constructively talk openly about what is wrong in the organization or their product. It is not enough for managers and senior managers to tell everyone they can talk openly and honestly - their actions must also allow the application of this practice. Different views must be permitted and considered, not quickly shut down.

Additionally, people must be able to communicate with a variety of other people without gatekeepers. In highly innovative software companies, such as GO1, all staff usually have a variety of communication tools ranging from instant messaging multi-chatroom applications, to internal social networks, to Wiki-type intranets which are not much regulated, allowing them to communicate more directly and more often with anyone they please.

Accepting and Driving Change

A large amount of excellent ideas will make no difference in an environment which does not accept change. Innovation only happens when change happens. People who are change-averse or who are "devil's advocates" too often actually hinder innovation. In an innovative environment, there should be no space for people constantly putting blocks on new initiatives (check the concept of Lean Startup if costs are of your concern).

Additionally, when hiring for an innovative organization or team, it is important to make a good effort to identify people who will have a natural role of internal entrepreneurs ("intrapreneurs"). These people are the ones who naturally accept and drive change themselves. Also, people with initiative must be recognized, no matter if they fail (more about this later). An environment that facilitates experimentation and rewards action is also essential for innovation.

Selflessness and Teamwork

Selflessness and teamwork, or something aimed at restricting egos that clog the innovation arteries, are also important values to have in innovative organizations and teams. People who fight to keep ownership of an idea will hurt the innovation process. Ideas need to change and evolve, and this can only be done in a team environment, with people of all types and backgrounds contributing to ideas and mutating them into something better and better.

Ideas need to be experimented with and, if needed, abandoned, radically changed or even 'pivoted'. It is all part of the process of achieving innovation and whoever holds on to an obsolete concept only to get the credit of it, will damage the organization and the innovation culture. Ideas are just the seed and these seeds need to mutate for successful implementation and follow through. And that is what really matters for actualizing innovation.

Courage and Acceptance of Failure

Courage is needed for standing up and promoting the necessary environment that fosters innovation, and also to withstand possible failure of initiatives. If people, and especially leaders, drop their energy and courage in standing up for these innovation-inducing values, innovation will not happen.

Additionally, failure is an integral part of the innovation process. The wonderful animated movie Meet the Robinsons (2007) shows this very well, for children and adults alike. Failure is a stepping stone to success, it is where pondering and learning happens. If people fear failure, or get punished by it, things will not be tried out and new ideas and initiatives will never come into fruition. Again, if costs are of your concern, check the concept of Lean Startup, which is applicable for new companies, internal organizational projects or even personal endeavors.

Autonomy

Autonomy is another important value, both for organizations which desire innovation as well as for individuals. As ideas need to be trialed and evolved, people need to be able to try their ideas and morph them without much restriction.

Lack of autonomy is one of the biggest blocks for innovation because it impinges and significantly delays trial and evolution. Innovation must move fast in today's world, and lack of autonomy puts a considerable foot-on-the-brake against it.

Continuous Learning

And finally, we come to the central subject of this chapter: learning and innovation. Although the link between them seems somewhat obvious, most people do not stop to truly understand the vital roles (and there are many) learning plays in the innovation process.

Learning is both a required building block of innovation as well as a consequence of it. There are many learning processes and styles, and all of them are important for innovation.

First of all, people can only be innovative if they have a diversity of information and knowledge to build ideas upon. As mentioned, ideas feed and grow from each other.

"All great minds stood on the shoulder of giants," as the saying goes. They all studied and acquired previous knowledge of a variety of their predecessors to be able to stitch concepts together, add their own experience, put a spin on it, and come up with a new concept. Knowledge, especially a good diversity of it, is essential to innovation.

Exposure to new concepts, due to continuous learning, always sparks new ideas in people's minds. This is easy to grasp when we think about our own experiences. When we learn, we have insights into how things work on the subject matter we are learning about. All these insights are new brain connections being created that allow us to think that way. All these connections will then become nodes upon which we can build other connections and nodes. The more you have of them, the richer your building blocks for creating innovative ideas. Think about Lego blocks: if you have just a few blocks, you can only create a somewhat limited variety of forms to play. If, however, you increase the quantity and variety of building blocks, you can draw upon them to create bigger, more diversified forms.

Also, the process itself of learning is practice for creating new ideas. If learning is the act of creating new neural-connections in our brains based on new information and experiences, it exercises the brain in creating those connections. As another saying goes, "our brain works like a muscle, in terms that the more you use it, the better it gets at being used." So, the more you exercise your brain with learning, the more apt it will be in creating neural-connections, which is the base for creation of new ideas as well.

Learning as a Force in Core Values

Aside from the neural connection between learning and innovation, we can identify learning as one of the underlying forces in all the core values for innovation we listed earlier.

When we talked about **diversity**, we talked about people from different backgrounds talking with and learning from each other. Learning here happens in two instances. First, each of these people have learned their own fields of expertise so that they can contribute to the group with their educated and different points-of-view. Second, once open conversation happens, their previously learned knowledge mixes and meshes with the other people's different knowledge and points-of-view. In this occasion, learning happens in between these people. They are learning from each other and the learning itself, those new neural-connections, is what causes insights into new ideas.

Also, **open and honest communication** promotes learning. Sure, learning can happen in any environment, but the degree and effectiveness of it depends deeply on the opportunity for people to have open and honest communication about the subjects being learned. The more opportunity for people to openly and honestly communicate with other 'educated' people on the subject, the higher the degree and effectiveness the learning will be. And as inferred earlier, the more learning, the more potential for innovation.

Learning also has a role in **accepting and driving change**. Change, which innovation requires, needs learning to happen. People are often resistant to change, as they need to get out of their comfort zone to go through it. They need to learn new ways of doing things and often new paradigms need to be learnt when change happens. Learning is the main way people process and cope with change. Creating a general attitude of being open to learn, as well as providing proper training in the new ways of doing things, are vital pillars in any change management situation.

Selflessness and teamwork have also to be learned before an innovation thriving environment takes place. It is natural for people to have large egos and to want to take advantage of situations. When we grow up, as children, we learn to share, to restrict our egos and to be nice to other people, so we can live a much better life in society. These things are learned; however many adults have not learnt them completely. Consequently, learning to be selfless and to work in teams is very important for promoting an environment ripe for innovation.

The same is similar for **courage and acceptance of failure**. It is not natural for many human beings to be courageous and, especially, to accept failure. These traits also need to be learned. Failure, especially, needs to be taken in perspective, and this needs training. Also, as explained in the 'Fixed vs Growth Mindset' theory (see Carol Dweck), people who have more acceptance of failure (Growth Mindset) learn better and achieve higher levels of success. It is in failure that we learn what went wrong and what can be improved upon. Failure also promotes learning on things that do not work and they often indicate new paths to follow or new challenges that should be overcome. As in a self-fulfilling prophecy, Growth Mindset can be learned and it is vital for innovation.

And finally, the need for **autonomy** has also to be learned by managers and leaders if they want their team to be innovative, and also happy.

As Dan Pink mentions in his excellent TED Talk 'The Puzzle of Motivation', autonomy is one of the three pillars of human motivation. Motivated individuals, with room for testing and trialing their ideas, are the ones who bring innovation to life. Many managers and leaders have grown up thinking that management and leadership are all about command and control. This might have been true in old militaristic organizations but in today's world, where innovation is not only desired but also vital, autonomy has to be the default option for trained employees.

Note the word 'trained' in my last sentence. For properly working in teams and in organizations, people must know what to do and how their work and actions will affect their colleagues, customers and other stakeholders. They need to understand what the team is trying to achieve and they need to learn their tools of trade first. All of these require training and learning. Once employees are properly trained and demonstrate proper knowledge in the subject matter of their work, they can be given autonomy. Autonomy, in this case, is both a reward for proper learning, as well as it is one of the underlying practices that fuel innovation.

Do not take me wrong by the last idea of having to train people before giving autonomy. I am very aware that many high-impact innovations came from people who were novices in the industries. People who came from a different background and did not have the old vices or restricting paradigms of the 'old ways.' This does not mean that these people do not need to be trained or given information when onboarding an organization, for example. It just means that, if the organization is open for change, has values of open and honest communication, and all the other innovations as well, those people, once understanding the current processes and what needs to be achieved, will be free to have autonomy to present and test new ways of doing things. Processes and paradigms should never be set in stone. Those innovation-driving values I mentioned are there to make sure they are not.

Formal and Informal Learning

So far, while discussing other aspects of learning and innovation, we have touched on two types of learning: formal and informal, both equally important for innovation.

Formal learning happens when training is conscientiously applied to or taken by an individual. It is important for innovation in the way that it gives people the building blocks of their trade or field of expertise. It provides previous knowledge gained by many other people before them. In this case, the knowledge is often tried and proved (although it should never be excused from critical examination) and should be taken in as fast and effective building blocks for innovation.

Informal learning happens when people perform activities themselves or when they go through experiences and/or informal conversations with other people. Informal learning is what happens in the coffee houses or in the company corridors. It's when people can mingle with other people and (as Matt Ridley mentions in his great TED Talk 'When

Ideas Have Sex') let their ideas have sex, which creates reciprocated learning as well as a sprout of new ideas.

The most creative and innovative companies in the world go to great lengths to promote informal learning for their staff. Take Pixar Inc., for example, the animation movie company responsible for revolutionizing the movie industry and considered one of the most creative organizations in the world. When Steve Jobs, one of its co-founders and at the time their CEO, wanted to build their headquarters, he brought in a world-known specialist to design a building that "promoted encounters and unplanned collaborations." The building itself had to promote informal learning. People and organizations that want to create environments that create innovation have to consider both informal and formal learning in their agendas.

Learning About Innovation to Promote Innovation

In order to create and promote an environment in which innovation thrives, people also need to learn about innovation itself. They need to learn that diversity, open and honest communication, accepting and driving change, selflessness and teamwork, courage and acceptance of failure and autonomy are all vital to innovation. They have to learn how to implement, practice and promote each of these values in their lives and in the workplace. Good courses and other learning material about innovation and about each of these desired values are essential for implementing and fostering innovation in people's lives and in the organization.

As we have seen, learning and innovation are intimately connected. Learning is both a requirement as well as a consequence of innovation. First, learning provides the building blocks of new ideas. Second, in order for people and organizations to promote innovation, they need to create an environment that allows new ideas to sprout and flourish. This environment is made of those values and behaviors that promote innovation. This environment can only be implemented through learning itself, as people need to come to know the importance of these values for innovation and they need to know how to live and breathe these values.

Chapter 3: Training through Storytelling

Everybody has a story to tell. It doesn't matter what your background is, we all have something to share that is a worthy lesson for another person. Whether you are working in a high powered corporate role or are a stay-at-home parent, we all use storytelling as part of our everyday lives. A compelling story can be the difference between selling your latest product or ensuring that your children brush their teeth every night before bed.

When people hear the term storytelling, sometimes the wrong ideas can pop into their head. Storytelling can resurrect memories of sitting up in bed with your parents while they read us our favorite fairy tales - but there's a lot more to storytelling than princesses and castles.

The art of storytelling is nothing new. It has existed for as long as humans have been living on earth, and over the course of millions of years the concept remains the same; but we have dramatically changed the methods of delivery. Our Neanderthal ancestors would tell stories about their adventures during the era that they were on earth, and as an art form the way in which we present stories may have changed dramatically, but the underlying concepts remain the same.

Storytelling is a great way to help people to make a connection with a topic or subject by presenting relatable situations that will encourage them to retain information. Think about it - how many times have you gone home and watched a documentary which has then enlightened you on something that you had no idea about before?

Modern storytelling comes in many forms. As society has evolved over the past few hundred years, so has the way in which we tell our stories. Starting with oral storytelling and storytelling through pictures, or drawings, we grew our audience with the arrival of print media. Early forms of newspapers changed the way that we communicated with each other, and eventually radio and television were the beginning of a movement that would redefine the world.

Television was a way to bring storytelling into the home, and a way for networks to promote the stories that they wanted the world to see. For around half a century, television was the main tool used for communicating stories to the public, but in the late 1980s the way we lived our lives was set to change forever with the introduction of the internet. The internet allowed the general public to then select the stories that they would like to read and watch, without being limited in content by the television networks or newspapers. With people now having the ability to choose which stories they ingest, the art of storytelling advanced at a rapid rate in order to hold the attention of their audience.

In the world of celebrities and pop culture, people enjoy watching stories about other people, almost more than they actually like going out and doing the same activities themselves! Bearing this in mind, it's no surprise that storytelling has managed to work its way into almost all aspects of our everyday lives. You don't just see a car advertisement any more - you are sold a story about how amazing your life would be with this new car. Even food and beverages are sold as experiences rather than sustenance.

How many times have we all seen advertisements for men's fragrances depicting a lavish beach setting with a young male having a great time while surrounded by a group of scantily clad women? Way too often. But these brands aren't just selling a fragrance, they are selling a lifestyle. 'Buy our product and you too can live this life' -

and as silly as that example sounds, it works! When that image is put in front of people on a regular basis, the next time we are standing in the supermarket looking to make a purchase, that brand always stands out on the shelf, whether it's for good or bad reasons.

When we think about the explosion of storytelling, especially over the past five years, it's not much of a surprise that we are now building our training and learning programs around similar concepts. If the general public has become so used to consuming information in a particular way, it's much easier to incorporate that technique into your practices rather than forcing a foreign concept upon them for it to not stay with them.

In this chapter, we will be taking a look at how to incorporate storytelling into your learning experience, without compromising the quality of your educational material. This can help by creating links between complex concepts and ideas, increasing our learner's attention by presenting information in a format that they are accustomed to digesting, and by appealing to a range of learning styles as opposed to just running with more mainstream learning techniques.

Storytelling can be a little more difficult in the training industry. Adult workers can be a lot more cynical about being emotionally manipulated. By nature, they are set in their ways and cautious about change, especially when things are going fairly well. However, when properly motivated, humans can effectively change, since it is built into our evolutionary biology. We just need to feel the urgency. It's up to us as trainers to be able to create the story that motivates learners and creates the urgency to develop a great learning environment.

Know Your Audience When Selecting Stories

Training and storytelling is not a simple formula that can be copied and pasted from course to course. A concise line may entertain or make an insight easier to remember, but to be remembered forever, a story must not only connect emotionally, but also connect to the right emotions. As we mentioned previously, advertisers are aware of this and work hard to connect to two fundamental emotions: greed and social acceptance, whereas political advertisers often stir up fear as the emotion to motivate. It's vitally important to know who our audience is, and to shape our stories to suit their demographic.

If we are training a group of teenagers on conflict resolution, we wouldn't use the same material to teach a group of corporate employees on the same subject, and vice versa. Audience is everything. If our training material is not tailored to our audience, we are at risk of the learners not being able to understand the content, or even worse, losing interest in the subject. Creating storylines for specific use cases in this situation is ideal. For the previous mentioned example, we would have separate courses for both groups of learners, tied together with a different story for each group that is more relevant to their current circumstances.

One step beyond ensuring that the stories we tell are appropriate for our audience is making sure our stories fit with who we are and are relevant. It's all well and good to be able to tell a great story that has your learners engaged, but we also need to ensure the story makes sense and is relevant to the course content. If not, why tell it? Make sure the connection between the story and the course content is clear for the learners. If this is not clear, your story may prove to be more of a distraction than anything else.

There is an art to telling a story. At some point, all of us have been at a party, gathering or bar and witnessed this in action. The storyteller has had the entire room captivated with their story. This is not necessarily because the story that they are telling is the greatest story that everyone has ever heard, but more to do with the way that they are telling it.

Anyone can run off the details of an event or anecdote that was mildly entertaining, but there is a huge difference between talking through the details of an event and telling a story. The person that has the room eating out of the palm of their hand is the person that pays careful attention to the pace of their story, using their tone, volume, and nonverbal cues to emphasize their points. Shifting a focus onto the key points of a story by building up elements and ensuring that the delivery of peak elements have a high impact is all part of the art of storytelling. It's about taking the audience on a journey and getting people excited about the narrative.

When we are telling a story in front of an audience, it is obviously a lot easier to emphasize these moments with the help of body language, tone and volume. But there are many ways to translate this into exciting eLearning elements too. Incorporate video and audio resources into your learning material to boost engagement and enhance your learning experience. By adding a range of media into your story, you are strengthening the core of your message, which retains the attention of the learner whilst providing the necessary ascension where required.

Why Planning is Your Most Important Step

Make the story short and to the point. Even a good story that goes on too long loses steam. Although it is great to embellish a story to build drama and drive home key elements, this can also have a negative effect on the learner if mishandled. There are a number of ways to keep your story on track, with the more critical being planning.

Everyone has their own method when it comes to planning, and like most things in life, there is no right or wrong way to go about laying out the foundations for your story. For those of us starting out on our storytelling journey, we will run through a couple of methods that you can use in your planning process.

Traditional Outline

This is a quick and easy way to plan the structure of your story, that can be put together in a matter of minutes. List out a series of key parts that you would like to include in your story that can then be arranged in order, allowing you to work through the flow as you progress.

These can be as simple as individual words or terms, as long as you know what they mean for your work. Bullet points are a fantastic quick and easy way to create structure for pieces and develop ideas, without diving into minor details that can be flushed out during the writing process.

Reverse Outline

Similar to the traditional outline, this is a great way to plan your story, working from the end or pinnacle of your story back to the beginning.

This method is perfect for planning the events leading up to your major event, and ensuring that you streamline the path to arrive at the destination.

Mind Maps

Write all of your ideas down in bubbles and then connect them via lines to arrange them around a central theme. You can use a mind map to chart anything your mind desires. It is, after all, a map of said mind.

Sequence of events? Character arcs? Exploration of theme? Story-world ideas? It's a very visual and hands on way to move around elements so that your story flows all the way to the end.

The Ugly First Draft

Just get everything out there and then clean it up later. As Ann Handley talks about in her book 'Everybody Writes': "Remember, you have to start somewhere and it's not always pretty. Sometimes the ideas start to flow once the pen meets the paper."

Get all of your ideas down. You don't have to use full sentences, you don't have to worry about grammar, just get everything down. Once you have that, you can then use your Ugly First Draft as a skeleton for compiling your final draft.

Be Aware of Discrimination in Stories

Remember that your learning material is going to be used by a wide range of people of varying backgrounds and cultures. Stay well away from any stories that make fun of any group of individuals, culture or belief. Make sure that you check your story for anything that could make someone uncomfortable.

Even true stories can embarrass someone if they were around when it happened. As an example, telling a story about a coworker who made a foolish mistake that cost the company a lot of money could be very risky if the incident is relatively recent. Or if the name of the associate who made the mistake is known, or if they have a friend, colleague, or relative taking part in your program.

The story has to be natural to the work culture of the group you are targeting. The players in the story should be archetypes that all learners within the group can relate to. The plot should provide opportunities for the learner to be the hero of their own story. And the story needs to set up a framework for the new skills and behaviors to be remembered.

Get Learners Involved in Storytelling

Stories are the most effective way to teach and they are constantly evolving. If you can get this balance right, the training becomes the stuff business legends are made of.

It's tricky to get the balance between entertainment and learning just right, as well as how to use just enough story with 'new skills' training. The story is there to set the stage for the learning experience. It's the core of the journey, not a quick stop along the way to serve as a distraction from the mundane material.

The most effective way for someone to learn a new skill is to have them involved in the learning process, as opposed to reading through a pile of material and then sitting an exam at the end. This is where storytelling can really help to make the learner feel like they are a part of the experience.

We have all seen methods around this approach floating around since we were kids. When I was in school, some of my favorite books were 'choose your own adventure' books. If you are unfamiliar with this concept, the writer would create a story, and at intervals throughout the story the reader would be given the choice for the characters to choose an option on how to proceed. This would then happen numerous times throughout the book, meaning that two readers could have two completely different journeys, with each journey following the choices of the personality type of the reader and creating a much more immersive experience for the individual.

A more modern take on this concept can be found in role playing video games. Based on the decisions that you make throughout the game, the story changes and no two people will end up playing the exact same storyline, unless all of the exact same choices are made by the player throughout the game.

This can also be easily implanted into your learning. Scenarios are often set up to lead to only the correct answer paths, when learners can learn just as much from making the incorrect decisions. You might ask, "why would we show the incorrect thing to do?" but it's actually a great way to play out a situation and show learners how the incorrect decision may impact their workplace. Once playing out the incorrect scenario, you would then return the learner to the point at which the incorrect decision was made, and they can then follow the correct path.

This can be used very effectively during Bullying or Sexual Harassment training, for example. Our learners may believe that it's acceptable to say certain things around their coworkers that they don't think are offensive. By taking them down a learning path that exposes how their actions affect others, and even their own position within the workplace, this can then have a positive impact and strongly reinforce the learnings, creating a process where information is much more likely to be retained and acted upon.

Another way to get learners involved in our stories is to give them the beginning of the story and let them finish it. Provide them with clear instructions on what you would like them to produce as it relates to the course, and let them fill in the gaps. This will prompt learners to think about how to jump from step to step, filling out the story in the process.

Without a story, you and your course can easily be forgotten. Stories help to trigger our memory. Compelling stories add context, history, and relevancy to you and your courses. They can make even the most mediocre things stand out and be seen in a different light. Stories add vibrancy and depth.

Treat your learning program like a brand. There's an exact science to a brand, and all good brands tell a story. Sporting brands do a great job with this. Remember the 'Be Like Mike' campaigns run by Nike? There is no way that any of us could possibly play basketball like Michael Jordan just by wearing his signature shoes, but their advertising made you think that when you put those shoes on and head to the playground that you could do all of the things that Michael could do. This created a huge following for the brand, turning it from a struggling tennis shoe company into the most dominant sporting brand in the world today!

A compelling story can be used to change the world, whether it's through a brand or learning, so we need to make the most of our opportunities to engage our audiences and create an immersive experience that benefits all involved. Also, remember why we are using storytelling in our learning in the first place - we are here to teach, not to preach. A surefire way to get an adult learner offside is by being too preachy with your storytelling. Make it about the experience, not the brand.

Chapter 4:
What You Need to Know to Achieve Engagement

Great, you've made the decision to take your learning or training online! Now you need to start creating your content. You may have been doing this for your classroom learning programs for a while, but aren't quite sure if you can use the same content and techniques when integrating your material with technology.

What might work in the classroom is not always the best solution for online courses, and there's the risk that you may spend days, or even weeks, preparing your course only to have low or no engagement from your audience.

We know that getting started can be hard and you no doubt have a lot of questions about what works best, how to get started, and best practices when it comes to online engagement. To help you out, we've dedicated this whole chapter to what we have found has worked best for us in the past. We'll share information on different types of media to include in your content, how to create it, and how to make the most of tracking and reviewing.

Getting it to Stick

Something that we all want to be creating is sticky learning. For those of you who haven't heard that term before, it means that your learners are interacting with your learning content, and remembering the information. While engagement occurs when learners interact with the content whilst completing your course, sticky learning is about having learners remember the content after completing your course.

Sticky learning is obviously the goal for any teacher, as it means that your students are not just skimming through content; they are ingesting and understanding it at the same time. This then allows them to apply their learnings to real life situations and isn't this why we are taking courses in the first place?

Success for learning doesn't necessarily mean that you have to walk away with a mastered skill. In fact, something that could be seen as even more valuable is that your learners walk away with a positive behavioral change or thought process. After all, sticky learning that doesn't result in a change in behavior isn't any more useful than something that doesn't stick at all!

So how do we develop learning materials that result in sticky learning? From our general learning best practices, we can see that everything reverts back to:

- Providing learning that has meaning for your audience and real life applications

- Engaging your learners with scenarios that speak to them

- Creating opportunities for your learners to share their personal knowledge and experiences with others

- Allowing users to participate in as many interactive learning experiences as possible, to get them thinking about practical application of skills

- Providing support to your learners and encouraging discussion and the asking of questions to clarify any topics that are not understood

- Initiating a post-learning experience in which students can keep in touch after completing the course, so you can see how the concepts that have been taught have been applied in real life situations (this is also great for improving your learning materials based on learner experiences and gaps in learning)

- Sharing results of your course - talk about your success stories and how those learners used your lessons and applied it to their everyday lives.

There is nothing new about any of these items we have talked about here. They are all things that we should already be doing, but sometimes we can get caught up in the material and forget that this is about the learner and not just the content. Hopefully by keeping these details in mind you can create a more rounded and sticky experience for your next course.

Bite-Sized Learning

There's some new buzzwords getting around the online learning community lately. 'Bite-sized learning' or 'microlearning' have been all the rage as the online learning platforms have increased in popularity over the past few years. But for many newcomers to the online learning world, you may not understand exactly what these terms mean, or how you can incorporate them into your programs.

The short answer is that bite-sized learning is about breaking up your course, or learning program, into a series of smaller, more manageable modules. This allows the learner to complete the course in short bursts, rather than having to spend hours at a time working on a particular part of their course.

In the age of modern technology, people no longer want to spend hours on end sitting at a computer working through a course. Instead, they would much prefer to be able to access their learning materials via a mobile device or tablet so they can learn at times that suit them - while they are in transit, waiting for an appointment, or simply when they don't feel like sitting at a computer.

The learning retention levels for bite-sized courses are much higher, due to the shorter length of the content and ability for learners to retain information, as they are not being overloaded with information in one sitting.

If you need any convincing that incorporating bite-sized learning is the way to go when creating your next course, let's take a look at some of the stats.

Microlearning makes the transfer of learning more efficient.

A 2002 study conducted by the BBC showed that learning in bite-sized pieces makes the transfer of learning from the classroom to the desk 17 percent more efficient. Let's take a look into why these efficiencies are taking place.

- When bite-sized learning content is easily and readily accessible, learners can take it at their own pace, wherever they are, and most importantly, when they are "ready."

- Bite-sized courses are more focused, meaning learners don't have to clutter their memories with irrelevant information - this makes retention easier.

- Learners have to digest only small chunks of information, making comprehension easier without spending too much effort.

- Microlearning content addresses only one to two learning objectives, whereas most courses yield four to five learned takeaways on average.

Eight out of ten L&D professionals favor microlearning because their learners prefer it.

According to the findings of a <u>survey on Learning and Development professionals</u>, 94 percent said that they prefer microlearning to traditional time-consuming eLearning courses because their learners prefer it (Boyette, 2012). Executives are also now realizing the efficacy of microlearning in addressing the needs of <u>Millennial learners</u>.

Millennials have a higher rate of engagement with their learning material when content is customized to their needs, on-demand and informal. Bite-sized learning has all of these points covered, making it the perfect choice.

Microlearning creates 50 percent more engagement.

Lack of stimulation and lengthy written pieces decrease the chances of success in an online course. According to a report by Software Advice, 'The LMS Features that Drive Employee Engagement Industry View,' more than 50 percent of the 385 employees who took part in a survey indicated that they would be more inclined to participate in extra training programs if the content was shorter.

They say that longer courses are not only more challenging to digest and retain but taking them also gets in the way of their daily work, which they are under pressure to complete.

Learning in stretches of three to seven minutes matches the attention spans of most humans.

To put it simply, we are not designed to spend hours on end focusing intensely on a single task. Humans are much more efficient working in short bursts, with time to digest before moving on to the next portion of content. Repetition also assists with retention.

Here's what a recent study carried out by the University of California-Irvine has found.

- Your employee works on a task for about 11 minutes before they are interrupted by a ring or ding of the phone, a popping email, or their co-worker who has come up to their desk.

- Within that span of 11 minutes, they engage in multiple short and quick tasks that average about three minutes each.

- If the task involves consuming digital information, they spend just 20 seconds browsing one piece of content before they click or flick through to the next.

The average learner has adapted to the world around us where information is delivered in short direct bursts, and our learning needs to reflect that behavior.

Bite-sized courses can be produced in 300 percent less time and 50 percent less cost than traditional courses.

According to learning architect Ray Jimenez, bite-sized learning courses can be produced much quicker and at a lesser cost than traditional learning programs. There's no need to pay for the instructor's time, buy or rent physical classrooms, pay for utilities, and spend money on classroom equipment.

It's a lot easier to create your content in shorter bursts and store everything online, saving on reproduction and lost time and money. It's also way easier to launch new programs, as the content is broken down into modules that can be rolled out independently.

Tips for Putting Together Your Bite-Sized Learning Course

Now you're ready to adopt microlearning, let's look at how you should be structuring your content for the most engagement.

Stick to one idea

The idea of creating content in bite-sized format is so that the learner can pick up a new skill in a short space of time. To keep things simple and on track, ensure to only focus on one idea in each course. If you want to run through a new idea, create a new course for that. By keeping the focus of your content in one area, you can teach your learners much more quickly and efficiently.

Engage

Just because your course is short, it doesn't mean that it shouldn't be engaging. If you start including sub-par content, your learners will be zoned out in no time. Kick your course off with engaging content, and finish it with engaging content - and keep it consistent with no 'filler' material in between.

Keep the content relevant

Further to the above information about engagement, it's important to keep your content relevant. This is bite-sized learning; you don't need to drag your points out. Keep your learning content simple and direct and your learners will be picking it up and understanding it a lot faster.

Be smart when grouping your content

Each module that you create should be focusing on a particular area within the core topic of the course. When creating your modules, it's critical to group your content in the correct module to ensure that the learning sticks with other content that it is relevant to.

Here are some tips:

- Determine the ONE learning outcome you wish to achieve

- Determine the tasks that are related to this ONE goal

- Identify content that is relevant to this ONE learning goal

- Arrange the content into nuggets

- Add knowledge checks that test learners for knowledge and skills they are expected to demonstrate in practice

Keep it in context

As content creator, your job is to present information that your learners can use. You can provide content with value and boost engagement by providing relevant content.

- State clearly at the start what learners will be able to do after they have taken the module.

- Fill your module with solutions. Show the learners how they can solve their real problems.

- Use the assessment tools to test learners for knowledge and skills that they will actually have to apply when they use the course knowledge in the real world.

Create a learner driven experience

The reason that you create learning content is so that your learners can learn, so why wouldn't you let your learner drive their learning experience. Give them the flexibility to learn when and where they want, create your content using a learning management system with a user-friendly and intuitive layout that lets the learner explore resources and discover content on their own - and don't forget to make it fun!

So how much content do I need for my course?

This is a tough one as every course is different and there are a number of things to take into account. The topic of the course, the audience that will be completing the course and their behaviors, the types of media that your audience is used to learning with and much more.

Obviously if you are creating a course on 'How to Cook a Roast Turkey' you may be looking at creating a lot less content than if you were teaching 'AngularJS for Beginners.'

The best guide when it comes to content is to follow the information we have mentioned previously in this chapter.

Start by outlining each of the key topics that are required to learn the information in your course. Break this information down into a series of modules, taking into account that each module should take no more than 11 minutes to complete to coincide with the attention span of your learners.

Once you have this list you can then see how many modules you will need to create content for within your course. A good bite-sized learning course needs to be exactly that, bite-sized. However, with more complex subjects that require a deeper level of detail, you can push out to a maximum of between one to two hours' worth of content, with six to 12 modules to break the content into easily digestible portions.

What should my content include?

Now you know what you are trying to achieve in each of your modules the next step is actually building out your learning content. There's a huge range of ways that you can do this and the driving factor behind what you should use lies within your audience.

Every audience will respond to different types of content, and determining this is the first step in deciding how you will present your modules to your learners.

In saying this, the most effective way to get the maximum engagement out of learners is to present your content using a variety of mediums, including interactive or immersive elements where possible.

For those new to creating content, some of the most popular ways to include content within online learning are:

- Video
- Interactive SCORM files
- Audio files
- Image based documents/slides

Ensuring that you are clear in your messaging so that learners can quickly and easily understand learning concepts is critical, regardless of the presentation medium. But now we will take a close look at each of these most popular ways of delivering content so that you can get the best engagement result possible.

Length of Video

When it comes to creating video content for online courses, the length of the video is critical in learning engagement and retention of knowledge. Jumping back to our section in this chapter around microlearning: short videos are much more effective for engagement, and for allowing students to absorb the content.

So how long should videos actually be?

There are numerous studies around this exact topic, with the optimal time coming in at between four to six minutes.

The team at edX have completed one of the most recent studies relating to video consumption in education, and they have revealed some very interesting findings.

The optimal video length is six minutes. While students watch most of the way through videos at this length, once you exceed that time period engagement drops off like walking off a cliff.

For all videos in excess of six minutes, less than one third of the content viewed is actually retained. In cases where a student is in a certificate-based course, due to that added commitment involved, this engagement time is lengthened out to 12 minutes.

The clear message from these studies is that content creators should be breaking their material up into bite-sized pieces to maximize on student engagement.

Interactive Content for Learning

Video is great, but getting your learners interacting with your content is even better!

Creating interactive content for the sake of interaction is not the solution though. Sometimes letting a learner absorb information can be better than sending a user on a clicking spree.

Understanding what interactivity in learning means can help you find the right balance for maximum engagement without resulting in distraction. The best way to understand interactive content is by comparing it to how you would interact in real life, in face-to-face social interaction.

Creating an experience in which an interaction results in a response, in the same way that a conversation flows, is the key to building a free-flowing online learning experience.

As we mentioned, forcing a learner into a click frenzy is one of the worst things that you can do. Excessive clicking leads to learner fatigue, which in turn provides more of a distraction to the learner than anything else. The focus becomes more based around clicking through all of the content as opposed to engaging with it.

Get the learner thinking, and then clicking to promote a deeper chain of thought.

Allowing your learners to think, reflect and feel the content is also a much overlooked aspect of interactive content. Stacking content that is forcing learners to push through everything at a rapid pace creates a rushed and stressful experience.

By creating space in the material, learners can take a step back, reflect on the content, understand what they have experienced and have a greater understanding prior to moving on to the next module.

Because you can't create a truly immersive interactive role-playing environment, think of ways that you can get the learner doing something similar within your course.

Allow your users to start practicing the skills right away. Creating scenarios based on achieving goals is a simple way of getting started with this.

Create a scenario, give them some background information, and then ask them what they should do. A great way to create this environment is to get started with text screens, followed by multiple choice questions that force the learner to think about applying what they know to a situation.

Having the learner create their own action plan to resolve a scenario is another great way to demonstrate knowledge. As the course progresses, get them to add to a document or form that will result in a complete process. By the time that the learner completes the module, they will have worked through the solutions as well as having completed their own action plan that is applicable in real life situations.

Mix it up!

Whichever path you choose to go down when you are creating your content, there is something that is important to remember - switch it up!

Yes, video is great - but an entire course of only video is going to be horrible for engagement. Include a range of media in your course. This may be a mix of written material, video, interactive content, audio and images.

Not every module needs to have all of these elements. However, if you create a flow between them over the length of the entire course you will find that learners will absorb a lot more of the content and be a lot more competent at applying their new skills in real life scenarios.

How should I test my learners?

So, your learners have completed their course, but now what is the best way to test them?

The most common online course assessment tools of recent times include multiple choice quizzes and 'match the answer' type questions. But these may not be the best solution for you.

Getting a little more creative with how you assess your students may provide a better form of measurement of success in your field.

Short and long form answers are great, but can be time-consuming as an assessor. Why not let technology make that easier for you? Try out some new tools to save time and ensure that your learners are actually paying attention.

Video response questions, and to a lesser extent, audio response questions, are great for this. Not only can the assessor quickly and easily view and grade long form answers, they can also see and/or hear students as they are responding!

As with content, changing things up is critical to engagement and getting the students to think in a range of ways as they respond. Hit them with the multiple choice questions in the early modules, and then wrap up the course with a longer form video response question or longer form style response.

Tracking Progress

Hosting your course within a learning management system allows you to track your learners every move.

See how people are interactive with content. If they are dropping out, see where the dropout occurs. If you have multiple courses, you can track enrollments. Most importantly, you can use the system to trigger email reminders and congratulation notifications as users hit milestones throughout the process.

How do I know if my content is any good?

So, you've created your course and you think it's pretty awesome, but you are still not sure if it's going to work the way that you hope.

Why not test it out?

Get some coworkers or friends to take the course and provide you with feedback. Encourage them to take notes as they complete the course, so that you know which elements might need tweaking, rearranging, or removing to create a better learning experience.

Another great way to test out your course is to release it as a Beta version to a small group of potential students. If you are charging money for the course, you may offer it for free to a limited number who are then required to provide feedback on the process.

The most valuable feedback you can get is from those who will actually be completing the course, so the more information you can get from your users the better.

After launching to the public, another great initiative to include is following up with all students after they have completed the course. This way, you can get their feedback around how you might be able to improve the course.

All of this feedback helps you to continually develop and improve your content, so you can attract more users and provide a more rounded and engaging learning experience.

Chapter 5: Informal Learning – Capturing The Unstructured

For a long time, there has been the idea that learning takes place formally, within fixed locations and predefined time spaces. The widespread understanding is that learning is only possible if there is a teacher or some form of instructor involved.

As we now know, this is not the case at all and some of life's most critical skills are learned outside of a classroom, and without a teacher being involved. Through the popularity of more subject-oriented concepts of learning, more diverse learning offerings and possibilities have started becoming readily available and more acceptable forms of education. It is now accepted that learning can take place outside of the traditional educational settings, which gave birth to the term 'informal learning.'

The term informal learning was introduced in the 1950s by Malcolm Knowles as he completed his pioneering work on informal adult education. Since then, many authors have written about informal learning and offered their unique perspective on the meaning of the term.

Informal learning provides a straightforward contrast to formal learning and suggests greater flexibility for adult learners. Being represented by a range of strategies including conversation, social interaction, teamwork and mentoring, informal learning involves interaction between people and is not limited to a predefined body of knowledge. We can simply define informal learning as learning that is predominantly unstructured, not taking place in a traditional institution of learning.

Informal Learning vs Incidental Learning

Informal learning should in no way be confused with incidental learning. Although incidental learning is a subset of informal learning, they are two distinct type of learnings with different meanings. Informal learning can be described as focusing on experiential forms of learning, whereas incidental learning puts the focus on unintentional forms of learning.

In this context, the learner may not be conscious of this learning as it is unintentional and occurs as a by-product of everyday experiences and activities in their daily lives. In comparison to informal learning, incidental learning can be a result of learning from mistakes or the hidden curriculum that may be associated with formal learning, suggesting that incidental learning is not a planned action.

Over the last few decades, the workplace has been increasingly recognized as a legitimate environment for learning new skills and knowledge, which in turn enables employees to participate more effectively in ever-changing work environments. Workplace learning includes experience-based learning, incidental and informal learning, self-directed learning, as well as formal organizational learning. Learning new skills and knowledge makes it possible for co-workers to manage change, perform well and be satisfied with their work.

For this reason, work and learning are synonymous, as experiences accumulate in the course of everyday participation in work activities. The work and learning experience encompasses the way employees make sense of the situations they encounter in their daily lives and especially in the work setting. If learning occurs as part of everyday experiences and participation, then there is also the potential for learning to occur in many different ways. This includes informal strategies, as well as formal learning initiatives that are associated with training.

While some structured workplace learning occurs, informal learning comprises the majority of learning. Informal learning occurs whenever people have the need, motivation or opportunity for learning. Most informal learning is tacit and taken for granted this is due to most people often only define learning narrowly. Most people still define learning with formal education and training, and assume that working and learning are two quite separate activities that never overlap.

What constitutes informal learning?

So now that we understand a bit more about informal learning, let's start taking a look at what some of the most common ways that we are all currently learning informally in our everyday lives - even if we might not be realizing it.

How many articles do you read on news or blogging websites each day? If you're anything like me then it's probably a lot! And that can range between anything from checking up on your local news, reading blog posts from industry experts or checking up on industry updates, or even searching through technical documents to see if you might be able to improve some processes within your team.

What you might not realize is that all of these things are actually extremely valuable forms of informal learning. It might not seem like you are learning at the time, but the information that you are processing as you read through these articles all contributes to improving your knowledge and boosting your career.

Also, how about all of those books that you read? Do you have a rapidly expanding collection of books that you're working your way through? Not all of them may be relevant for you to learn something applicable to your career, but you can take lessons from anything and apply it to your situation. Books are one of the oldest forms of informal learning that are often forgotten, while getting mashed into the formal learning landscape at the same time.

Another outlet that has long been considered more of a time waster than a valuable resource for learning is social media.

Yes, you can get sucked into the drama and time-wasting if you choose to go down that path. However, if you start making the most of your network and tapping into the knowledge of your friends, colleagues, peers and industry experts, you can actually learn a lot more than you think. The ability to share articles on Facebook and LinkedIn allows for you to pass on material that you find useful to your friends, while they in turn can do the same for you.

Facebook is a tricky one due to the less professional nature of the network, but LinkedIn is a goldmine for finding new and exciting material that is relevant to your industry and recommended by your peers. But if you really want to tap into learning through your social networks, head over to Twitter.

Twitter may seem like a confusing mess at first to the uneducated user. But there's no doubt that once you get up and running and using the network to its full potential, it's the most useful tool for finding out new information online.

The key to learning through Twitter is all about building the right network that can provide you with the information that you need to learn. How do you do this? By following the right people. Following colleagues and peers is the best way to get started, but the beauty of Twitter is that you can also start following those people who are leaders in your industry, or people who are currently in a role that you aspire too. You can see what they are reading, what they are sharing, and learn more about the topics and articles that they are getting involved in to advance their careers.

There is so much information online these days that it can be hard to know what is worth investing your time in. Having the recommendation of these influencers is a great way to ensure that you are only reading quality material and not being sidetracked by sub-par distractions.

YouTube and other video-based websites are another great source for informal learning material. TED Talks, conference presentations, interviews with experts - these are all incredibly valuable pieces of media that can be learned in just ten minutes. You'll learn things you can apply to your career that might have otherwise taken months, if not years, to learn through your standard traditional workplace training programs.

Another great way to join aspects of both formal and informal learning is by attending meetups, trade shows, conferences and similar type events. By networking with those who are actively trying to innovate in your industry you can gain masses of knowledge through having a simple conversation with the person standing next to you.

While some people may believe that conferences are a waste of time and you are better off saving your money, this couldn't be further from the truth. The connections you make at these events, coupled with the sharing of knowledge that takes place between all attendees, can allow you to access some concepts that can be applied to your business within a short amount of time.

Where would we be without the internet? Pretty much all of the above items, plus many more, can be found on the internet. You can look up pretty much anything at any time to broaden your knowledge on even the most niche field.

Tracking and Sharing Informal Learning

I was recently speaking at a event in Silicon Valley about social learning and how the often ignored aspect of informal learning is not considered to be 'real learning.'

At the end of the session an older gentleman raised his hand during question time and stated: "But you can't get a certificate for informal learning, so why should we be focusing on it?"

I replied with, "Yes! You're exactly right, but did you get a certificate every time that you finished a book? Or read a technical paper?"

Looking at things from a management point of view, he kind of had a point. How could managers track, and more importantly, facilitate the sharing of information that their employees were learning?

Well, there are some exciting new tools on the horizon that will be a game changer when it comes to capturing and sharing our informal learning experiences.

For example, at GO1 the team have been developing a new tool that can sit right on your internet browser to assist in highlighting articles and pages that you would like to recommend to your network.

The way that this tool works is by having learners create a learning profile on the GO1 website which contains their learning information - everything from industry of employment, books read or currently reading, online courses taken and created, and the option to follow other users.

This 'follow' option allows users to then follow people of interest in a similar way that LinkedIn does, except you can see all of the learning activity of that user. This makes planning and advancing your career a lot easier, as you can follow learners who are in the position that you are working towards to see what they are currently learning.

The best part about this tool is that it also comes with a Google Chrome Extension and sits right on your web browser. So whenever you come across a website that has some really interesting information you'd like to share with your network, you can simply add it to your profile through the extension. Then whenever anyone following you visits the website, they will get a notification that points them to the information that you have flagged!

This turns every single page on the internet into a potential learning item.

Your user profile can also be used as a record which has captured all of the informal learning that you have completed. You can then share that with your current or future employers to show them what you have been studying to improve your skillset.

Recognizing Informal Learning

Informal learning might not have been taken seriously in the past, as demonstrated by the gentleman at my talk, but these tools could be a huge step in the right direction of tracking and quantifying the learning that is taking place in non-traditional locations.

The value in this type of learning is through the roof. And due to the fact that informal learning allows the user to establish their own direction when it comes to learning and building their knowledge, the engagement - and more importantly, retention rates - for these programs are substantially higher than that of the programs allocated to learners by their employer or an instructor.

Just as new workplace trends such as remote working and flexible hours are still having trouble becoming commonplace with organizations across the world, the acceptance of the value of informal learning may take more time. But at least we are starting to introduce the concept and begin educating more people on how it may be able to help them.

The Acceptance of Informal Learning

As the recognition of informal learning increases, it is no longer regarded as an inferior form of learning whose main purpose is to act as the precursor of formal learning. It needs to be seen as fundamental, necessary and valuable in its own right, as people need to face more challenges throughout their days and are looking to develop new skills that may not necessarily be able to be taught in a traditional setting.

With people constantly being faced with challenges in their workplace that have an effect both on the way they perform their job, and their participation in office culture, it is important that we are being equipped with sufficient knowledge to complete our jobs to the highest level possible. This will also allow us to access opportunities to continually increase our skills and improve our abilities.

Nowadays, organizations are no longer relying solely on technical skills, but are placing more emphasis on competencies in other areas like knowing how to learn, problem-solving, creative thinking, interpersonal skills, ability to work in a team, communication skills and leadership effectiveness. These skills are seen as crucial skills to have in order to face the challenges in a world where workplaces are evolving so quickly - and those that refuse to adapt will be left behind. These so-called 'soft' skills can be acquired through incidental learning, which forms a part of informal learning, and is primarily derived from social situations.

People may have little control over when or where this type of learning occurs. More specifically, this learning may occur during the process of performing other activities and may be more incidental than informal.

We are now expected to continually modify and update our work practices through many different learning channels in order to sustain competitive advantage, remain employable and perform well within our role. Therefore, all workplaces should be increasingly recognized as a legitimate environment for learning new skills and knowledge that enable our fellow employees to participate in everyday, work-related learning opportunities. If learning through life is essential to the labor market, then workplaces and employees are crucial in supporting, valuing and developing opportunities for learning.

Rusaw (1995) describes how the opportunities for informal learning inherent in membership in professional associations can have a positive impact on all involved in the process. Professional associations serve as a place to identify a mentor, with mentoring relationships providing a great source of informal learning for both the protégé and mentor. In addition, the opportunity to serve in a position of leadership (such as an officer, chairperson, or task force leader) allows members to gain a perspective on management processes and practices by doing them.

Learning opportunities that extend beyond the barriers of an employee's job description may offer exposure to knowledge, skills, and abilities required for future assignments, and/or opportunity for promotion.

Creating an Environment to Promote Informal Learning

The exchange of information is a crucial part of informal learning in the workplace, and it is seen by many as the essence and the core of informal learning which will help add value to those participating. Activities such as reading and study groups can serve the purpose of facilitating informal learning in the workplace.

It's very easy for employers to support these initiatives by providing meeting spaces, resources to purchase books, and even the reward of food if the discussions are held during employee lunch breaks.

What kind of information should be exchanged though?

Information that will add value and enhance the knowledge of the attendees are what we are trying to achieve, so creating and facilitating activities to enhance that (for example, software to simplify tasks, information and learning resources, how to handle workplace problems etc) is the ideal outcome from a management standpoint.

With the advancement of technology, the exchange of learning and information no longer needs to be done face-to-face and in real life. All of these activities can also be done virtually through distance learning and online discussion. Online communication tools are increasingly used in the business world to allow teams and their members to communicate freely, no matter where they are located geographically. With this framework already in place, the opportunities to communicate with your wider team to learn from them is an easy and cost-friendly step.

An informal learning approach provides a great opportunity to create processes that assist in monitoring and optimizing the development of human resources for organizations looking for innovative solutions, and to set harness on its productive potential. For a lot of small businesses, having a permanent human resources team is simply not a cost-effective solution, so finding an easy-to-manage solution is the ideal outcome.

The human capital view of informal learning is a pathway that seeks to align both education and work. In part, this alignment is why interest in informal learning, particularly in the workplace, is growing quite dramatically. Once employees become proficient in the basics of the job, informal learning helps employees expand the scope of tasks they can handle and the efficiency and effectiveness with which they do so.

As employees become experts, informal learning helps them deepen their expertise, and as employees outgrow their current roles, informal learning helps them identify possible new jobs and begin the process of preparing for them.

Informal Learning Does Not Replace Formal Training

It is important to note that informal learning is NOT a replacement for formal learning, but rather, should be used to complement formal training. The most successful way to implement informal learning is to allow it to co-exist with formal learning.

Although some people may think of informal and formal learning as separate from one another, these two are interrelated. There are multiple ways for combining formal and informal learning to develop skills for today's workforce. The most common practice for entry-level employees (apprentices, trainees, cadets and interns) is to combine or alternate learning acquired in formal off- and on-the-job training with informal learning acquired through everyday experience on the job.

The key to the success of such programs is the extended on-the-job experience obtained in a supervised environment. Innovative approaches include 'fully-on-the-job' programs and 'learning bays' which locate both formal and informal learning at the worksite.

For existing employees, the most popular strategy is to blend learning acquired in informal (often in-house or external training programs) with on-the-job practice and experience. Alternate strategies include action learning approaches, which provide opportunities for employees to get together to share information and develop suitable action plans for quality improvement initiatives, business innovation, and self-help for users of newly introduced or critical technologies and products. This also enables learners to practice skills in simulated environments before being expected to apply such skills in the real workplace.

In the long run, businesses will make their choices according to their own evaluations of what will suit their particular companies or strategic directions at the time that learning is required. And choosing the right way to apply the advanced training that your business needs could be the difference between adopting a culture of improvement and success, as opposed to ending up stagnant and losing your best team members to your competitors.

Where Do We Go From Here?

There's no doubt that informal learning is going to play a huge part in the future of professional development. But what should we be doing as managers, to make the most of technology and integrating this into our organizations?

The first thing is always to remember that informal learning should be used in conjunction with a more formal training program. This may mean that once every month employees may be given a formal training program to complete. This could be an in-person training session or an online course - or even a combination of the two. Once this program has been completed, in order for the employee to complete the module, additional tasks can be set out over the weeks to follow containing a series of informal learning tasks.

Theses could be as simple as 'read five articles on topic X', 'find the application of X that is currently being used in industry Y' and so on. This provides the basic framework for employees to start thinking about how they are learning outside of the workplace, and sometimes when they don't even realize that they are learning!

By introducing these concepts through a formal process, this will then set in motion the thought process on how the learner can continue to learn and advance their knowledge through small daily exercises like reading through a website, or even scrolling through their social media feed for information that might be relevant to them.

Like anything, once these new behaviors are established, it becomes easier and easier to maintain and build off.

Chapter 6: Beyond Gamification: Creating Real Motivation

For some time now, there has been a growing discussion about gamification and how it is changing the way that the world learns. Yes, it's true that gamification is making a serious impact on the learning industry at the moment, but why is this happening?

Like any concept that starts to rise in popularity, there are going to be a lot of critics speaking out against the new and different thing making an impact on their world. But a lot of people forget that while gamification may seem like a relatively new concept, it's actually really an old idea: creating feedback mechanisms that can motivate and stimulate interest. And creating feedback loops and mechanisms to motivate people is not a new development.

Biologically, we have been hard-wired to respond to the world around us, and modern technology is now putting these age-old behaviors to use. Advancements in these technologies over time has allowed gamification to develop at a more rapid pace than ever before, but when it comes down to it, the underlying concepts are exactly the same.

The typical examples given for the genesis of gamification is the rise of digital games over the last few decades. Most people reading this article have probably used a Nintendo, PlayStation, or Xbox console, or even just played Solitaire or Minesweeper on a Mac or PC. More broadly, whether it was board games or console games, everyone grew up playing games. And games are becoming more and more pervasive. You can't walk down the street, or go online, without having the latest ad for Game of War or Clash of Clans shoved in your face from every direction.

At times, you might not even realize that something you are doing is a part of someone's gamification process. They might be all turning into app-based systems now, but if you look back in a few years, when you opened your purse or wallet how many rewards cards for various food or beverage outlets would you find? For example, the coffee shop reward card that had three stamps as you worked towards getting ten stamps and a free coffee, or the sandwich shop card where you could earn enough stamps to get that free lunch.

We were all guilty of it, but the system worked. How many times did you go to that coffee shop to get your stamp, when in reality, the coffee was actually pretty average, just to edge closer to that one free drink?

A simple rewards program can play a major factor in building brand loyalty and spending habits. Even when the end reward is not of major value, that chance to get something extra out of your purchase drives customers to 'make the most of their spending' by remaining loyal to a brand.

One of the largest examples of gamification that we see in our everyday lives is through financial institutions.

There's no arguing that banking is big business, so acquiring and retaining customers is more important than ever. This also means that 'stealing' a competitor's customer base is also high on the agenda, and offering rewards on new credit cards is one of the most popular methods for doing this.

I'm not sure about you, but every time I'm online, I am hit with an ad for the latest credit card deal. Whether it's extra frequent flyer points, cash back, or balance transfer bonuses. These are all forms of gamification to get you in the door. Once you're in though, you have to spend thousands of dollars before you see even the smallest return in points or cash back; but once they have you signed up, the battle is already won.

When we turn the conversation to gamification in learning and technology, we need to utilize the concepts that already exist in our everyday life and have already proven to be a leading developer of behavioral patterns.

The leading tool associated with gamification is notifications. From the second we wake up in the morning the first thing most of us do is look at our phone, where we can find a screen full of notifications prompting us to look at things, complete tasks, or respond to people. With that, the next logical step in education was to incorporate these dual concepts into our learning processes.

Today notifications are a part of everyday life, so why don't we start using notifications and badges in our learning processes? Well, we are!

There are many examples of digital rewards and notifications that apply to productivity applications rather than just gaming applications. In fact, our modern lives are filled with notifications and alerts.

A great example of notifications is in health and fitness. With the introduction of the health services to the core iPhone functions, almost everyone has now got some form of app associated with tracking steps, fitness and their other daily activities. Even though there might be hundreds of these apps on the market, they all lead back to one core function of using notifications to engage with the user. If you have been sitting at your desk for X number of minutes, you receive a notification telling you to get up for a walk. If you are behind on your daily fitness goal, you will receive a notification suggesting some of your favorite exercises.

How can we apply that same concept to a learning situation?

You have created an awesome online course, and in total it is going to take the learner around four hours to complete. Getting a student to sit down and complete a four-hour course isn't going to be an easy task, so let's break that four hours down into 15 minute modules. Once we have our bite-sized modules ready, we can set up notifications that remind the learner to complete a module on a daily basis.

If our learners are only having to spend 15 minutes a day on a module, reinforced with a reward for completing their daily task, they are much more likely to keep up with the program and engage with the content, than if they were forced to complete the whole course in one sitting.

In a world full of distractions, the effectiveness of bite-sized material and notifications is amplified. It doesn't matter what you are encouraging your audience to do, when used properly notifications have the ability to continuously engage and encourage behaviors that lead to a faster rate of learning and brand loyalty around your product.

Notifications have become the modern-day equivalent of your nagging mom who would tell you to get off that damn video game and finish your homework.

Interactive notifications can spur all sorts of new behaviors

Some of these can be simple like sending a message or enrolling in a new course, but they can be a powerful tool to keep learners engaged and wanting to learn more! Think about all the ways that we experience notifications on a day-to-day basis. We get a notification that we have just received a new email or SMS – or perhaps an alert from Facebook or some other app on our phone. What do we do? Of course, we open up the app or game straight away and interact with it! We have become trained to follow the notifications.

Following on from our previous example of breaking a course into bite-sized modules and using notifications to remind our learners to complete tasks, you can create new learning behaviors with your notifications. There are a lot of games out there that will provide players with a reward of in-game coins or cash just for logging into the game each day. This creates a behavior where the player is coming back every day to collect their reward. There's no reason we can't adapt this to learning.

One key component to ensuring notifications work effectively is timing. If you receive a notification during the day while you're at work, there's a very strong chance that you are going to be busy and ignore it, with the intention that you'll come back to it later. How many times have you ever come back to that thing that you said you'd come back to later?

We need to target our learners at times when we know they are more likely to have their phone in their hands already and are able to spend 15 minutes quickly completing a module. While it would be great to encourage people to learn while in transit, 95 percent of Americans are currently driving to work instead of using public transport, meaning they are just as likely to skip over your message as they would be during business hours.

If we set our notifications for the evening when we know that people are home from work and relaxing watching TV, we are much more likely to get them to engage with us. By this stage of the day they have decompressed from the work day and feel more mentally free and ready to learn.

Over a period of time this will then develop into a routine for our learner. They will know that their notification for the next module is coming, and they will be looking forward to it. After a while, just like any game, the participant wants more and it's at this point that we need to be suggesting new courses and ways to keep students involved in actively learning. This could be through enrolling in new courses, being involved in webinars or discussions or even recommending to friends. The important thing is to use the learning behavior and keep the content coming.

We might not think much of them, but interactive notifications can have a dramatic effect on our learners.

Badges or rewards don't need to be something big or over the top - even the smallest piece of encouragement is enough to push a student to remain in the top of their course results, or tell their friends about how much fun they are having with their course. After a few days of working through their program, users begin to want to collect more points or badges, and not only that, they want to collect all of the points to gain access to the best rewards. This sounds nice and simple, but it's not that straightforward.

We need to create an experience to match the badges

If a user spends two hours reading through a wall of text and then receives a badge, is that really going to encourage them to come back for more? Make your content fun and engaging, and tie the content to your badges. Make the most of being able to include mixed media in your learning.

Video as a form of learning is much more likely to keep the learner engaged, with a recent study showing that even the slightest improvements in the production quality of the video can have a dramatic impact on the user. Everyone has access to a good quality video recording device right in their pocket these days, and with a few production tips and editing in a program like iMovie, you can now produce your own learning videos.

Learning through mobile devices is at an all-time high at the moment, so providing content that is easy for people to digest while on their mobile devices is important.

Audio is another forgotten form in the learning world. Everyone has their favorite podcasts that they listen to every day, so why not take your teaching into the podcast space. Include audio modules that are interacting with other modules. Like video, it's easy to be able to record and edit video to a very high quality with very little knowledge of the space, and course creators should be taking full advantage of this.

It's important to match our notifications setup to the needs of our target user base.

If we are teaching children, obviously we will be setting up our notifications in a very different way to that of corporate learners. Because if we don't tailor to our target audience, engagement is going to suffer.

Understanding our audience is the key to this. How many notifications are too many, and if we send too many notifications will it drive our learners away?

Working with younger learners, we are able to send more notifications reminding them that they need to take actions on certain items. The younger generation are used to receiving a barrage of notifications every day and thinking nothing of it. However, if we did the same thing with our adult learners they are likely to get frustrated by so many notifications coming through and turn them off altogether.

Unfortunately, there is no simple formula that we can look to that will give us the answer to how many notifications is the correct amount, but we can look into what we previously talked about in creating behavioral patterns and go from there.

With Great Notifications Come Great Rewards

So, we have our notifications set up. Now what is the incentive for our users to be clicking on them and interacting with us?

Depending on your audience, your rewards are going to vary. The most common rewards program that spans across almost any industry is the points-based system. We are all familiar with this, and are probably involved in more than we can remember at any given time.

A simple solution, a points-based system works great across a range of industries due to the flexibility involved. We can set up a number of tiers at which users can redeem services or products for their points. It's nothing too exciting, but it does help to factor into that brand loyalty that we've been talking about.

How can we make rewards work for online learning though?

There a number of ways that we can add areas to earn points within our online training programs. We can add points for enrolling in courses, completing modules, inviting others to courses, creating course content and much more. The question is then, what do we do with our points?

In an environment where a course marketplace is available, users could use their accumulated points to gain access to courses at no cost, or be given exclusive access to reading material or documents that can only be unlocked after reaching a certain level.

Another great incentive for users is by having a leaderboard. Even when no reward is on offer, just having a leaderboard for your team is enough to get the competitive attitudes kicking in and pushing people to out-learn their colleagues to hold down that number one position.

Usually with a leaderboard situation, at the end of a set period the leader is given a prize of movie tickets, a restaurant voucher or something similar as a reward.

Online learning rewards don't have to be redeemed online

A common misconception is that rewards are just creating a fictional facade of achievement rather than actually being of value to the learner. This does not at all need to be the case. Just because rewards points are earned online, that doesn't mean that our users should have to claim their rewards via online features.

Make your rewards something that people want. If you are the administrator for your team, you can easily come up with some really fun things that are inexpensive and will motivate your team to push harder to win.

Some of the simple rewards that can be used for smaller teams might see the individual points leader for the month earning additional leave or leaving early on a Friday. You could also offer team rewards in the form of lunches for collectively reaching a certain goal and encouraging each other to contribute.

That's fine for small teams, but what about when your team contains hundreds of people within larger organizations?

A number of large corporations have built stores specifically for rewards programs that their employees are involved with. This can best be done by partnering with outside organizations. Offering credits at websites like Amazon, Asos, bookstores, restaurants and more is a great way to get people inspired. They are earning real items that they would like to purchase and by learning they are saving money in doing so.

Who's Doing It Right?

DuoLingo has been teaching the world new languages for free with their own crowdsourced text translation platform. The platform is designed so that students can learn a language while translating text-based documents. Beginners start out with easy to recognize, short sentences, and as students advance they receive more complex sentences. As you progress, so does the skill level required to translate the document.

For each learner, DuoLingo provides the learning and translation tools to assist the student in recognizing and understanding the words they are reading. You can even vote on the quality of another student's translations as a way to provide a feedback loop. Top rated translations, as voted by the students themselves, are then displayed for viewing by the public.

As learners progress in their new language, points are accumulated as lessons are completed or documents translated. Lessons that involve a skill are then completed when a given number of translations are finished. Given that general content taken from online sources is a lot more interesting than text designed purely for translation purposes, these assignments prove to be much more engaging.

DuoLingo also have a number of time-based skills points where correct answers see the learner progress much faster, whereas incorrect answers slow you down from moving up levels and involve additional exercises to get back on track. The system tracks a student's every move and provides them with feedback on how to improve their development. This great functionality leads to a great education gamification experience.

Another company who are doing a lot of things well at the moment is Ribbon Hero. Ribbon Hero is available as a free download from Microsoft, designed to help tech users of Microsoft Office know how to make the most of their ribbon toolbars. This is another great example of using gamification to educate while simultaneously updating users on products.

After installing Ribbon Hero, you can easily initiate the game from within any of the Microsoft Office programs including Word, Excel, PowerPoint, and more. Once you have started the game, you are awarded points for completing tasks as you work through the 'ribbons.'

Ribbon Hero have arranged their challenges into some key areas based around the ribbons within each program: text manipulation, page design and layout, artistic presentation, and a more generalized quick points section.

With the text editing, page design and layout and presentation, the challenges are designed to guide us through all of the key features within each area, as we set out to edit a sample document. The quick points section doesn't offer specific challenges, but lists features instead, which can be used outside the game to accumulate points. Over half of the available points must be earned through three areas, with users earning the chance to make up the remainder of the points by developing their skills outside of the walkthrough.

Microsoft have done a great job with Ribbon Hero by creating relevant and engaging exercises for their users in short lessons. The exercises, while not too hard to complete, push the user enough to explore new functions and as a result become bigger fans of the Office range of products and more attached to their functionality.

One of the greatest features in Ribbon Hero is its ability to track its users to provide further training in areas that the user might not be focusing on. In turn, this is pushing people to explore more of the Microsoft products and opening up the door to encourage individuals to use Office programs for tasks that they are currently looking elsewhere to find efficient solutions.

When we think of social sharing, Microsoft Office isn't the first thing that jumps to mind, but with Ribbon Hero they have done some great work to ensure that users have full social integration with Facebook and Twitter. This means that users can then share their success with their friends, in turn promoting the Microsoft brand. As one of the best corporate education gamification examples out there, we tip our hat to you on this occasion Microsoft.

Make Your Learning Fun

The culture at every company is very different, and to truly provide an effective gamification experience you need to do your research to create an experience that works well for your audience.

What has worked for DuoLingo and Ribbon Hero in our examples above might work for their users, but your experience may be a lot different, and need some fine tuning. However, the core models that have been used can be replicated and set in place as a starting point.

When trying to make learning fun for your users, there are a few basic questions that you should try to answer to get started.:

- How are users interacting with my platform, and how can we turn that into a rewards-based experience?
- What types of rewards would drive my audience to complete more tasks?
- How can we track/distribute rewards?
- What can we do to scale gamification as we grow?

Once you have a plan for how you might be able to tackle each of these items, it's then time to put your plan into action and start implementing some rewards-based experiences with your users.

Remember, it's best to start out small and to keep things simple, and then once you find out what is working and how users are interacting with things, you can then start to build off those behaviors to further develop your concepts.

As we have discussed, adding gamified elements to anything is a surefire way to increase engagement and grow your user base.

So, what you are you going to do to make your platform more fun?

Chapter 7: New Age Educators

As the education and training world further tightens its grasp on embracing online learning, we are now not only seeing a substantial impact in the way that students are consuming their educational content, but also in the way that content is being created and distributed online.

This rise of interactive media in the educational world is not anything new. In fact, over the past five years, many college and universities across the world have noticed a rapid decrease in the number of students attending lectures on campus - instead opting to watch the video of the lecture which is posted online at the completion of the session.

Having this flexibility at their fingertips, students can maximize the use of their time rather than losing hours of their time in transit, which could be used much more effectively for further study, or preparing coursework relating to the lecture they have just watched.

This is fantastic news for educational facilities everywhere, as the space they need to operate can be drastically reduced as attendance drops off and they can push out more of their learning material online.

But this has also opened up another aspect of learning that may spell the demise of the traditional classroom teacher.

What Does it Mean to be a Teacher?

It's one of the oldest and most important professions, as recognized in every country and culture throughout the world. But what it means to be a teacher is evolving. We have always known our teachers to have completed many years of training through the college and university system, followed by practical experience in the classroom.

Our teachers were educated, with a wide range of knowledge across a wide range of subjects. This prepared them for the onslaught of questions of students, and having to adapt to teach a range of subjects that they might not have a background in studying – or may have no interest in wanting to teach.

The day of the 'traditional teacher' may well be numbered though, as technology has now opened up the doors of being an educator and allowing anyone to produce educational content. Yes, colleges and universities are always going to have highly qualified educators preparing their online content, but we are now seeing the rise of the new age teacher who has no classroom, or actually any experience teaching, being able to create effective and engaging learning material.

Subject Matter Experts vs Generalists

Unlike our traditional educators who have learned to cover a number of subjects to allow them to expand their capabilities and be a more attractive candidate for positions within the education system, the new age teacher is a generalist. They know one subject, and they know it inside out.

The rise of subject matter experts as teachers has become more commonplace with the rise of the popularity of bite-sized learning and online courses.

People no longer want to sit through a long and extensive training program that covers a wide range of subject matter relating to their area of study. They want to be able to break their learning experience down into short, very specific, targeted segments that they can learn as individual components - then over time put the components together to form a more rounded knowledge of a subject.

We most commonly see subject matter experts conducting online training programs in topics related to the tech industry, where education can be broken down to be program-specific, and even to being able to perform a task within a program.

Most people have done a few short courses on something to do with Microsoft Office, Adobe Photoshop and a whole stack of other software provider materials. But most of the time these courses aren't even made by the software companies; they are produced by individuals who are subject matter experts on the programs.

The rate that the tech industry moves is phenomenal, and being able to keep up with that pace as an educator is a daunting prospect. So when someone creates a new piece of software, what is the best way to get your team up-to - scratch on learning how to use it?

Create your own short course for everyone to use. This may have previously been done with a user manual, but now that creating courses is so quick and easy, a simple course could yield tens of thousands of enrollments, educate your users, and save you time in updating manuals that will be out-of-date by your next release.

Embrace the Modern Way of Learning

As we've already discussed, the role of the traditional teacher is diminishing with more and more students opting for shorter courses compared to the more traditional classroom-based learning environment.

Over the past five years, we have gradually seen an increase in the amount of technology in the classroom for both students and teachers.

From the teacher's side, it started with losing the overhead projectors, and then the much-loved TVs and VCRs. Now, a laptop connected to a display through a projector or other type of screen is the norm.

When it comes to students, gone are the masses of textbooks, folders full of paper and much-loved graffiti-covered pencil cases packed full of pens, pencils, highlighters and all of the other essentials that were staples for a pre-2000s student. These days, every student has a laptop. Assignments are submitted online and notes are taken and lessons are circulated via online tools. To be honest, as a young technology enthusiast who hated having to write anything down, but would happily type out stories for hours on my PC, I wish things had been this way when I was in school too!

If you're going to be teaching in the modern world, you need to embrace technology and work on the assumption that over the coming years, the way that learners will be consuming their learning material is going to drift further away from the traditional methods, to be more focused on mobile learning through the use of tablets, phones and other handheld devices.

Bearing this in mind when designing any learning material, it's critical that you use a platform that can easily be translated - or converted into - content that's readable for any sort of device.

Creating Learning Content Has Never Been Easier

Forget your lesson plans, and having to go through the process of teaching the exact same material over and over. You can now quickly and easily create your entire course online!

Remember only a few years ago when building your own website was a task so daunting that you would pay someone thousands of dollars to do it for you? Well it's still not a complete walk in the park for those of us who are less technologically minded. But over the past few years we have seen the rise of platforms such as WordPress and Squarespace, which have made creating your own website as simple as dragging and dropping objects onto your screen, allowing even the most design challenged users to create their very own professional looking website in a matter of hours!

I know you're thinking 'that's all well and good, but we don't want to build websites, we want to teach people!', But what if you could apply those ~~very~~ same design principles to creating your very own online course?

Well now you can!

Course creation tools are starting to appear on some of the top online course websites across the internet. While these tools are still in the early stages of their evolution, some platforms such as GO1 are advancing their course creation experience at a more rapid rate than others. This allows more people, who don't have the technology skills needed to create courses on their own website, to quickly and easily drag content into place using a similar format of that which we are used to using on Squarespace.

The key with this process is still always going to be preparation. But once you have got all of your content ready to go, it only takes a matter of hours to get your course set up, and for students to start enrolling.

You start by creating a new course, and then within that course you break your content down into a series of smaller modules to cover the key topics within your courses. It's within these modules that you add your learning content.

Similar to the tools you are familiar with on Squarespace, you can upload a wide range of media to be included in your courses - this includes, video, audio, PDFs, documents, spreadsheets, interactive learning items (SCORM files) and much more! You can simply click the 'add' button, choose the file type you'd like to include and hit 'upload' and it's all ready to go. Once you've got everything uploaded, you can then also drag the learning items into the order that you'd like them displayed.

It doesn't just stop there. You also have the ability to add in your own assessments at the end of each module too. There is a really wide range of assessment types that can be selected, so there is something ready to go that will be relevant to your audience. These assessment types can include simple grading techniques such as multiple choice quizzes, matching the statement to the answers, listing out answers, or you can get into more detailed responses requiring the assessor to review, such as video/audio response questions, long form answers, submitting assignments and more.

One of the most exciting new features currently being unveiled leverages xAPI technology, in which you can take any video from YouTube and then set it up to stop and ask the viewer a question, waiting until they select the correct answer before continuing. It's quick and easy to create assessment tools like this that are transforming the way that we create courses.

The Classroom Teacher that Took His Program Online

After spending many years as Principal Teacher at a TAFE institution in Australia, Chris Murray has now embraced the world of online learning and uses his business, Jacaranda Lodge, to develop training materials in leadership and supervision for the hospitality industry, specializing in the use of exemplars.

Prior to moving into the world of online teaching, Chris was a novice when it came to technology. He knew the basics around how to use his email, look things up online, and how to use the Microsoft Office suite to prepare documents as required. But he was in no way confident with using technology, let alone feeling like he could build and sell his own set of courses aimed at the hospitality industry!

Chris was an early adopter of the GO1 course creation tools, which allowed him to very quickly create his own customized learning content. Originally releasing 'Jacarandas: A Hospitality Case Study' in print format, Chris was looking to take his training online and creating a course that was available online was the perfect solution for distributing his learning material.

Due to his extensive experience in the classroom, Chris says that the most notable adjustment that he has had to make is communicating with the students regularly to understand how they are progressing, and learning how to guide and anticipate answers so he can provide help when needed.

One of the toughest things to design when it comes to online learning is create engaging and meaningful assessments. Chris tells us that getting students out of the habit of the 'tick and flick' mentality can be a huge challenge.

"My favorite feature of the GO1 system is that immediate feedback is provided to students when they sit their assessments. They are given an instant result."

Even though he had the interaction with his students in the classroom, being able to monitor progress and handle questions was still very limited, and once out of the classroom he really had no idea what his students were working on.

Having the ability to follow the journey of his students as they work through his courses has changed the way that Chris interacts with his students. And by enabling real-time chat functionality, his students can now talk to him and their fellow classmates to get the help they need - when they need it.

Chris tells us that one of the main reasons he started creating his print resources before they ended up online, was that he was teaching students from so many different language backgrounds.

A strength of the resources he created is that they use exemplars, both good and bad, of decisions that need to be made in a supervisory situation, which creates a much higher engagement rate and results in a higher rate of retention for the learning material with the students.

"If a student can see a logical pathway to work through a problem, it slows them down from rushing into a torrent of words in a written assignment which they do not understand."

In the current Australian education system, online learning requires the teacher to be familiar with, and able to facilitate, learning from the wealth of online materials appearing on the internet, which is a huge step forward from the traditional textbook-based programs of the past.

"I have received a number of enquiries from people who wish to set up a similar business to mine, and the online materials will enable me to point them in the direction of 'Leadership and Supervision for Hospitality' which will enable them to get started."

Chris Murray is a great example of how to adapt traditional learning concepts to online courses, and we are very excited to hear about how he has been progressing his content based on the demand and results of his course.

Give Learners the Help They Need, When They Need it

We have become so used to being able to get anything that we want with the click of a button, including customer service or help. As we touched on in the previous chapter, adjusting from a traditional learning environment to taking your learning online presents a different set of communication challenges than we are accustomed to. However, this can also be easy to resolve.

Just as the way that we get learning content has evolved, so has the way that educators want to interact with their students. On-demand assistance has never really been an option for the classroom, as once you leave you are essentially on your own - with the exception of the occasional email, which can sometimes take days to get a response due to the masses of enquiries an instructor may receive.

Just as we are used to with anything else online, online learning is now developing an 'on-demand' culture where students can get the answers they need, anytime day or night, through an online community within their course.

One of the best social tools to assist with completing learning content is a forum style discussion that can be accessed while completing a course. These discussion areas or 'groups' are great for not only the students, but also the instructors, due to the style of discussion.

By allowing all students completing a particular course to interact, and ask each other questions as they move through their coursework, we find that in most cases the other students in the course can answer questions raised without needing the instructor to get involved at all.

This alleviates one of the toughest aspects of being a teacher, and also allows learners to build a community around the subject of the course to further expand on their knowledge of the topic, and even potentially cover new aspects which may not be covered in the coursework.

Universities are Not Going to Disappear

So now that we understand that anyone can be a teacher with the help of educational technology, does that mean that we are going to start seeing universities disappear?

Not at all. Well, at least for the moment.

You see, even though anyone can teach, that doesn't necessarily mean that they are going to the best person for the job. As an example, would you like to learn more about Roman history from a professor who has been teaching the subject for 20 years, or from someone who has read half a dozen books on the subject and has completed a short course about Julius Caesar?

Quality and experience are going to be the defining factor when it comes to not only keeping educational institutions alive, but also, being able to set a price for your content. In the age of YouTube, it's easy to be misled by under-qualified educators, but this is not something that you will ever need to worry about when it comes to attending a university.

That said, the way that universities are now functioning, online course work does make up a large part of the syllabus. Lectures can be viewed online, assignments submitted, notes downloaded and so on. The average time of attendance required to complete the average degree has reduced dramatically, with students only needing to commit a fraction of the time to the classroom, while completing the bulk of their coursework from home.

Understanding that they need to adapt to survive, educational facilities know that by having the freedom for students to learn in their own time, in a place that is comfortable to them, they will continue to be a sought-after destination for people looking to develop new skills.

What Do Our Future Educators Look Like?

Well now that our educators can come from all walks of life, the face of learning is starting to change. Age and experience are no longer a prerequisite for being a 'good teacher' and the community in general prefers to learn from a subject matter expert on a topic, rather than a generalist.

The growth in popularity of bite-sized learning also means that our subject matter experts don't necessarily need to be compiling lengthy course plans or courses to span over a number of months, which can be a very draining and time-consuming process. Now, they can simply direct their focus on teaching a group a very specific skill in a short amount of time - sometimes as short as just one hour!

These short courses mean that courses are more direct and to the point as opposed to covering aspects of the topic that might not be as critical, but traditionally have been added to provide a more rounded knowledge of the topic at hand.

The ability for more teachers to be present in the community, both online and offline, is a great asset for the world as it also means there are going to be a lot more subject matter experts teaching a wider range of subjects than we have ever seen offered before.

For example, if you want to learn how to play Christmas songs on a ukulele five years ago you may have needed to find a teacher running a class that you can attend. Today, you can simply go online to an online course provider such as GO1, enter your search term, and instantly have access to a number of courses from different providers that you can enroll in with the click of a button.

While playing 'Silent Night' on ukulele might not exactly be your thing, the same process can be applied to pretty much any topic that you can think of that you would like to learn more about. This not only opens up the world of learning to the student, but it also exposes the educator to a large audience of students that might be interested in enrolling in their courses.

Any way that we look at it, the face of education is changing. And while it might seem a little scary, the possibilities that this will open up for everyone who is interested in learning new skills, or helping others to learn new skills, makes this one of the most exciting times for education that the human race has ever seen!

Chapter 8: Implications of the Knowledge Economy

The words of consultant and management educator, Peter Drucker, have never been truer.

"The rate at which an organization learns may become the only sustainable source of competitive advantage."

How do you then maximize learning in your organization? With the world changing so quickly, how do you ensure your organization has the knowledge to be at the forefront of resolving challenges and is making the most of your opportunities?

Traditionally, learning is thought of in terms of 'teaching' by a top down approach, presenting content to your employees using courses created by a manager or a third-party provider. This approach is proving to be increasingly insufficient to cope in the new knowledge economy.

The way that we learn has changed dramatically over the decades, and will continue to evolve as we move forward. One thing that we do know is that top down learning is a thing of the past. The increased access to learning materials with the growth of the internet has spawned a new type of learner. And with the world of education at our fingertips, we no longer want to spend time in traditional learning settings being force-fed information that isn't relevant to our needs or interests.

As we discussed in the first chapter of this book, the way in which we learn now is much more informal than we have seen in the past, and the content we consume is in a shorter form than traditional learning material. Once upon a time everyone within a department would undertake the same training programs, but now we have learned that to get the most of our talent we need to have individual training programs for our employees relevant to their role, personality and strengths.

The Current State of Learning

At the moment, research shows that 94 percent of learning buyers believe that the working style of employees is dramatically different today than that of the past five years - and that new approaches and technologies are needed. When the same learning material has been used for the past decade and been effective, making the switch to modern technologies can be a scary thought.

Who is going to spend all of that time updating the materials, and then training staff on how to use the new systems? It may be a scary thought, but the longer companies delay the decision to embrace modern learning tools, the harder it's going to be to make the switch.

Up to 67 percent of managers currently consider 'ease of use' to be the biggest issue when selecting a learning management system. There are currently hundreds, if not thousands, of learning management systems on the market, but choosing the right one for you could be the difference in saving a lot of time and money or causing you some extreme headaches.

Not all of these systems have the same offerings, so it's important to do your research to ensure that the product that you are signing up for can fulfill all of your needs. Whether an LMS is easy for you to use or not can very much come down to the set of features that you are looking to use within the system. The functionality within an LMS can vary dramatically depending on the system, so you'll need to do your research and find a system that is not only easy to use, but can handle all of the complex learning problems you're going to throw at it.

The way we work is also changing. The age-old life plan of going to school and getting a job that you'll spend the next forty years working in is a thing of the past. These days, if an employee has been at a company for more than five years you would say that they have been there for a lifetime.

By 2020, half of the workforce could be contingent labor rather than employees of a company. The growth of remote teams has led to a dramatic increase in contingent labor in the form of contractors, who are reducing costs for companies whilst still contributing to the business in the exact same way as the person sitting next to you in an office has done in the past.

Given the increase in contractors needing to be trained on company practices and standards, it is critical that we have a solid plan in place for distribution of knowledge. Contractors aside, we can't forget customers, franchisees, or suppliers - who also need to be a part of our knowledge base. With so many people needing to access your knowledge base in order to operate a successful business, ensuring that your knowledge delivery service is not only easy to use, but reliable and engaging, becomes vital to your growth.

Learning is moving to the forefront of the talent management product stack. Learning now motors the talent strategy for onboarding, engagement, motivation and succession. The more that we can educate our talent and provide them with the skills that they want to learn, the more engaged they will be, and in turn more productive for the company.

Learning and development teams should work to cultivate strong learning cultures within their organizations to retain and upskill their team members. More than half of all Millennials expect employers to provide them with learning opportunities relevant to their job. Employees who derive meaning and significance from their work are more than three times as likely to stay with their organizations, reporting 1.7 times higher job satisfaction and 1.4 times more engagement.

It is estimated that 73 percent of learning is informal. This means that traditional learning structures and systems are missing out on the largest piece of the pie! The more that we embrace that learning doesn't need to be a defined process, the sooner we can adjust to new concepts. Take an apprentice for example. Yes, they do spend time attending school to learn their trade. However, the balance in this arrangement is generally one day of school to four days of on-the-job learning.

It's in these situations that mentoring programs become even more important and teach a wider variety of practical skills in a short amount of time than any formal training program. Setting up a mentoring program is an easy task. Make the most of the experience within your company by assigning your junior team member a senior mentor to work alongside. Even if no official time is set aside for learning, giving the younger team member the opportunity to ask their mentor questions about their projects, clients, and even life in general is more valuable than any training program.

That direct feedback doesn't just help in upskilling team members, it creates a culture of shared learning within the organization that will assist in boosting team moral and developing a culture of trust and respect between all employees.

Improving Your Learning Experience

Our learning experiences have become very analytical, just like the rest of our lives these days. We can track and measure every component to see what is working, and how we can make improvements to systems or processes. There are currently two areas that research is showing can cause a dramatic improvement in our learning experiences across a range of organizations - by up to ten times. These areas are instant access and informal learning.

Let's start by taking a look into instant access.

The use of mobile devices has been increasing at an incredible rate over the past decade. They have overtaken pretty much every aspect of our life from shopping, reading and even watching television and movies. The thought of being separated from their mobile device could send today's youth into a breakdown of epic proportions. Having users rely so heavily on their devices has its advantages for the learning industry though. As long as they have a device in their pocket, people have a tool connected to every learning in existence!

Taking into account this connection to devices, it's no surprise that mobile has now become the device of choice for users, with over 51 percent of people now opting for their mobile device over the more traditional laptops or the PC. And the gap is growing each month.

This translates to more people looking at vertical screens on mobile than horizontal screens on laptops and desktops. So, we have to adapt if we are to survive. Having a mobile-optimized learning platform is no longer a luxury - it's a necessity. Not only that, but it needs to be a functional, easy-to-use platform. We can get away with a lot more clutter on a website because we have the space and people are more likely to explore the pages, however with our mobile devices, our screens are only ten percent of the size at best. Using a clean, easy-to-navigate program has become more important than ever. We shouldn't have to teach our users how to use a learning system; they should be able to simply pick it up and start learning.

You Shouldn't Need to Learn How to Learn

What's the first thing that you do when you need to learn information about something? You head to Google. We have become heavily reliant on Google for telling us all of the answers to the questions that we have in life. The answers to all of life's great questions (including how to cook risotto, fix my car, and tie a tie) can be found with the click of a button.

So why wouldn't we have a search function within our learning platform? We are already conditioned to search for the answers we want, and have developed a behavior of learning through searching, so it's only logical to include a strong search feature within our learning materials.

Learning does not just occur at a course level. Learning can happen outside of your courses, and providing an environment for our users to learn and ask questions can be the difference between completing a course and completing a course and actually understanding the content.

Not all learning needs to be done through a training program or course. You can be exposed to new knowledge in your field on a daily basis simply by interacting with your co-workers. Some of the best things that we ever learn will come from our work colleagues, just by observing or asking them how to complete tasks. This is where mentoring programs come into play and can prove to be just as valuable as more formal training programs.

Finally, learning should be a simple and fun process. As we said above, you shouldn't have to learn to learn! You should be able to simply pick something up and start learning, without having to worry about how to get to the learning part. Most of all, it should be fun, after all isn't that what we all want? To have fun?

In the previous chapter on Gamification, we ran through some great ideas on how to make learning programs more fun and engaging - because if our learners are having fun, they are more likely to absorb the content we are presenting them with and walk away wanting to learn more! Creating a culture of fun learning experiences leads to an innovative and progressive organization which benefits everyone involved.

Mentoring programs walk the line between formal and informal learning, as they are part of a formal program but are provided via informal access. But let's have a look at some more aspects of informal learning that can boost the efficiency of our training programs.

It's estimated that 75 percent of learning is informal. The required learning might be a subset of a course, but you can learn just as much from your co-workers during the day as you will in your training programs.

We've all heard the saying 'content is king,' but for learning professionals, those who generate the content are really the ones in charge. This doesn't have to be the case. You have an organization packed with incredibly smart and talented employees, so make the most of the knowledge that they have! No one person or team should be held accountable for creating an entire company's training program. Collaborate with your co-workers to create amazing and unique courses based around the skills that they have.

Increasingly, users themselves are generating content, and the outcome is much more relevant and engaging learning material.

Everyone has a unique skillset, and tapping into that knowledge base doesn't only help in educating others within your organization, it also pushes the teacher to become even more of an expert in their field and bring the team up to their level.

Another big advantage of having teams collaborate on learning material is that we are building a library of content specifically for our company. This means that we can brand things our way, promote our company values, and essentially allow our employees to experience a learning program that allows them to be immersed in their organization's values. And in the end, we are saving a lot of time and money outsourcing our development to individuals outside of the company that might not understand our values, ending up with a cookie cutter course that all of our competitors are also using.

Learning can be a collaborative and shared experience. There's no reason you need to be isolated or sitting in silence as a group while you are learning. Learning as a group is a great way for people to interact and ask questions, opening up the discussion on topics that might not otherwise be covered.

Given that we are now doing the majority of our learning online, it becomes vital that we provide the opportunity for our learners to have the same open discussion experience as if they were sitting in a classroom. This can easily be created with the help of discussion group or forum type platforms, allowing users to interact and ask questions to not only their tutor, but other students. We will then be opening up the opportunity for informal learning within the group, which can also be used as a great resource to find out what your users want to learn and giving you a jumpstart on your next round of learning material.

The way we present our learning material can have a dramatic effect on our users.

The retention rate for information for text-based information has been documented to reach around ten percent, whereas video-based content reaches up to 65 percent! By the year 2017, it is estimated that 74 percent of all content on the internet will be video-based, and within one year of that we are set to jump to over 80 percent.

The time to be embracing video is now. Everyone has a personal video recording device in their pocket, and it's become easier than ever to record and edit together your own professional looking content without spending days trying to figure everything out. Make sure you are getting that high retention rate by including video content in your learning material.

This isn't to say that everything that you produce should be video-based. Definitely, still utilize other forms of media in your programs, but ensuring that video is a core element of our learning materials will guarantee that we have the attention of our learners.

We also need to remember that the current generation of employees entering the workforce are more technologically advanced that their counterparts of five years ago. They have grown up on a healthy diet of video games, devices and technology evolving at a rapid rate, and are quick to adapt and learn new skills without sitting through lengthy training programs.

Millennials have also become used to complete personalization and being delivered only the information that they want and need. This is actually a great lesson for us. Why should we be learning about something that's not relevant to us?

Today's learning buyer believes in building a learning process that's a win-win for both the organization and the employee. Creating customized learning pathways for each employee is a simple process that involves only selecting the courses that are relevant to one particular employee or role within our organization, to ensure that we are not wasting time and money on training that is not required.

It's not only wasting time and money; it's also wasting engagement.

When we start working through a course that isn't relevant to us, our attention instantly drops. As we prepare for our next course, before we even start our attention level is now diminished as we arrive at a part of the course that is critical to our role.

Personalized programs ensure that we are only exposed to the content that is relevant to us and our needs, and keeping our energy and engagement levels high.

Even though things are trending towards these newer and more versatile learning models, the more traditional formal compliance-driven learning programs still have a role in the market.

Due to regulations becoming more onerous across the world, it is even more critical to keep our employees up-to-date with current codes. Training for compliance can also be turned into a fun and engaging experience, but should not be brushed over or rushed through purely for the sake of meeting compliance regulations. As we all know, failure to comply with regulations can result in hefty fines, and in some cases, it can result in endangering the lives of both employees and the general public. Learning professionals have the tough task of navigating both worlds to ensure that they cover all of their bases.

It's a 'dog eat dog' world out there, and when we are trying to win new projects the competition is fierce. With two out of three organizations saying that demonstrating compliance is very important to them, the difference between winning or losing that big new contract could come from your training program.

Having a compliance training program in place isn't just about avoiding lawsuits and making sure you can continue to operate as a business. It also comes down to showing your customers that they can trust you and rely on your organization to handle their project in a professional manner.

Keeping on top of compliance training can be easy with the help of a learning management system. We are finding that one out of every two organizations are currently relying on their learning management system to demonstrate compliance, and provide training for their employees.

Bearing this in mind, it is vital when selecting a learning management system that you choose a system that can cover the needs of your business. A number of platforms may advertise courses that cover topics that you are seeking compliance in. However, they may not be accredited courses and can potentially leave you wide open to lawsuits.

If you are wanting to cover compliance with your learning management system, you need to be sure to check that any courses you need to complete are recognized with the authorities relevant to your industry. This is not only important for accreditation, but also for your employees who are completing the course. If they can have a certificate of completion from an accredited course, this is furthering their professional development and allowing them to take their training with them from team to team, and job to job as their career progresses.

Now, more than ever, it's becoming more important for learning and development teams to work to cultivate strong learning cultures within their organizations. A direct result of this is that we will notice a shift in our teams where we are able to retain and upskill our team members.

Setting up employees with professional development plans ensures that your staff know they are progressing their skills. Up to 58 percent of employees say that being involved in a professional development program contributes to their job satisfaction. This is not only going to let them see the path that they are on for their training for the near future, but it also helps to keep them engaged with their role. A recent survey of the American workforce by

The Energy Project has revealed that employees that derive significance from their work are three times as likely to stay with their organization, reported 1.7 times job satisfaction and are 1.4 times more engaged.

Now we can see why we need to have great professional development plans in place for our teams. There are many tools available to help create this through learning pathways. Through a learning pathway, you can set up a series of courses that are relevant to an employee's role, and over time they will work through each of those courses to complete the pathway. Learning pathways can be set up to suit a person in a specific role, or can be completely customizable from employee to employee.

Employee Development isn't a One-Time Thing

One of the worst things you can do is have your employee development program as a one-time sit down that lays out everything for your staff - and then you don't talk to them about it again for another year. As a minimum, managers should be holding one -on -one meetings with all team members at least every six months to set out their development plan. This should include discussing courses that management would find beneficial, courses that the employee would like to do, how this will affect their role and career development, and where they would like to be after completing the program.

Having all this information within a learning management system makes this whole process much easier to manage. If you use the right system, it's simple to create your own customized courses to suit your business needs and match your branding, all while having access to a marketplace of courses covering a wide range of topics. This ensures that employees will never be stuck for choice when trying to improve their skills, and at a fraction of the cost of traditional classroom style training programs.

Chapter 9:
What Does the
Future Hold?

It's an incredibly exciting time for learning and technology with the rate that things are progressing with our selection of learning tools. We are currently in the middle of the mobile learning phase, which has changed the way that we learn, and given us access to learning materials anytime anywhere. But things are about to take an even bigger jump forward.

Virtual reality (VR) is here and it is evolving at a rate that will see most homes across the United States owning a VR headset by 2020. Looking back a few years, if you were looking to get into the VR game you were going to have to part with in excess of $500 to get your hands on an entry level headset. That is no longer the case.

While the high-end VR devices are still not cheap, pretty much all of the leading gaming and technology companies are now releasing their own affordable versions of virtual reality viewers. We have Google's Cardboard VR headsets, as well as Samsung making headsets that you can simply insert your phone into, to create the virtual reality experience for less than $50 – which is really changing the game. At a price like that, VR has gone from something that we would all like to try out, to something that everyone can now experience.

Virtual reality is a huge move in the right direction, with the introduction of a fully immersive learning environment. Once you strap on your headset, you have no choice but to be fully focused on what you are seeing and hearing throughout the experience. At this stage, learning applications for this type of technology are still being developed. However, it's my opinion that VR will only take us so far, and won't be used to its full potential as the popularity of augmented reality continues to rise and is more adaptable to real life situations.

Time to Embrace Augmented Reality

Taking things one step further is the introduction of augmented reality (AR). Still in its infancy, augmented reality is going to change the way that we live our lives. Whereas virtual reality lets us experience another world, augmented reality lets us interact with the world that we live in, as a virtual layer sitting on top of everything we can see.

Both VR and AR are set to be the future of learning. Imagine stepping into an online classroom and completing exercises, interacting with other students and asking questions all from your own home.

Over the past few years, virtual reality has established itself as the next step in entertainment and gaming. The principals behind the technology are simple to understand and even brands like Sony are banking on the technology, as they try to enhance the gaming experience through their PlayStation system.

Augmented reality, on the other hand, is still a relatively new concept that the general public is only just starting to embrace - and one of the main reasons they have learned about it is due to a bunch of animated Japanese creatures appearing all over their cities!

That's right. The PokemonGO craze that took over the world in 2016 was the first time that most people had experienced any form of augmented reality. Some people may argue that what this game was enabling wasn't exactly AR, but it allowed the public to grasp the concept and understand what this type of technology is capable of in the future.

So, what exactly is AR then? For those of you that have not yet had the chance to experience augmented reality, here's a quick rundown of how it works.

Imagine being able to see the world just as you would any day, but then having an additional layer on top of what you can see that is helping you to interact with elements, or see information about the items you are looking at that are updating in real time.

At this stage, the experience still requires you to wear a form of glasses to be able to see the overlays. We have seen a few versions of these starting to hit the market already with the most primitive form being Google Glass, and the most recent release being the developer version of the Microsoft HoloLens. With time, it's expected that rather than having to wear glasses, a user will be able to access this form of technology by inserting a contact lens onto their eye, or even having an injection to permanently install a chip into your eye.

So How Will Augmented Reality Change the Way We Learn?

Imagine being able to train your employees on dangerous situations or simulating emergencies without ever putting anyone in danger. This is the future of training.

The immediate training impact will be seen in industries where there are many dangerous moving parts in the workplace, but the classroom will also see huge improvements. Being able to place screens or interactive objects around a room will allow instructors to achieve a highly immersive learning experience without even being present in the room.

Each student now has the opportunity to have their own teacher to interact with in their field of vision, guiding them through exercises and allowing them to be completely absorbed in the learning experience.

As an example, let's take a look at worksite or fire safety training. With AR, you can have your students standing in their workplace with a number of hazards being simulated and overlaid on their environment at any time. This not only forces the user to be immersed in their training program and completely understand what hazards might look like, but it also allows them to complete the program in their very own building - so that should an incident occur in the future, they have already lived through the escape and handling protocols. As opposed to listening to someone talk about them, watching a video, and fumbling their way through a poorly organized fire drill once every quarter.

Augmented reality is an amazing breakthrough for the regular student or worker, but it's even more of a breakthrough for students with special learning needs - such as those with hearing impairments. All learners can now get the attention that they need, in the form that will help them the most.

The introduction of this technology will not only change the way that we learn, it also changes the way that we communicate with each other.

Gone will be the days of video calls, as the technology that we have seen for years in movies, with interactive holograms projected into our living rooms, is now a reality. Skype is already on board to take communication into the

21st century, with integrations for the HoloLens already in place. And it won't be long until this is the standard when it comes to keeping in touch with each other.

AR is probably going to be the biggest game changer we have seen since the introduction of the mobile device, especially in the manufacturing industry. A company called Meta has already developed technology where employees in the manufacturing industry can learn how to create elements, by using Minority Report style systems that allow users to interact with the device via body movements, and dragging virtual items onto real world output sources such as printers or production lines.

The next phase of gamification and interactive learning is set to blow our minds. We are going to be able to design training programs that allow students to be involved in virtual situations and guided through the process. We are still a long way away from having the resources available to develop programs that will allow us to develop courses of this caliber, but it is coming, and probably sooner than we think.

The Introduction of Consumer Learning

As we have continued to introduce technology to the classroom, the term 'blended learning' was coined to represent the integration of traditional learning methods with technology. Over the past few years this has proven to be one of the most effective teaching methods, yielding a much high engagement rate than focusing wholly on either traditional or online learning.

As this concept has evolved and become the norm in education, the next step is for this to fall into the retail sector, where organizations are trying to package their goods with the required training programs to use them.

Think about this: when you currently buy a product, how do you learn how to use it?

Nine out of ten people would answer by telling you that they would look up a tutorial or help video on YouTube. Now this is all well and good, but this is a huge missed opportunity for product producers or resellers.

And who are these people teaching us how to do things? Are they experts? Probably not. Do they actually know what they are doing? Possibly, but there's no way to be sure.

So why aren't retailers providing training along with their products?

As an example, imagine purchasing a new makeup or beauty kit. The kit contains everything that you need to create the same look as shown on the advertising material used to sell the product, but the missing link is knowing how to actually use the products to create the look yourself. Sure, there might be a one or two-page guide inside the box, but that's not going to do the trick.

So rather than letting your customers head to YouTube to get advice from an amateur on how to use the product, why not combine the product with the training required to use it.

This can work in one of two ways.

The first being that you are selling the product, and included in the package is the information to complete an online course to teach you how to use everything in the package, as well as giving users access to a community of users who are actively responding to queries on a message board or forum.

The second way to do this is by selling the training package, and by signing up you get the product for free.

This isn't a new concept by any means, and people have been selling courses that include products for a long time - but generally these are in-person courses with instructors and not online courses that you can work through at your own pace at home.

The benefit here is that your customers are now receiving the training provided by an authorized instructor to achieve the outcome as desired by the company, as opposed to getting a great product, and then being taught how to use it by a sub-par teacher.

Obviously, this concept can be applied to a huge range of products across a wide range of industries, but combining a good product with a high-quality training program provides a new level of engagement between customers and products.

Personal Learning

With more and more options becoming available to access learning materials every year, more people are starting to take learning into their own hands rather than relying on other people to provide them with the help that they need.

Traditional educational facilities such as universities are always going to continue to exist and evolve, but the age-old path of going to high school, then university and getting a job is starting to break up.

As startups and other small businesses are starting to become more common, and the sought-after career path for many Millennials, young people are no longer wanting to spend three or more years in a classroom - only to learn that when they graduate and start looking for jobs the skills they have just learnt are already outdated.

Technology moves fast, and so do the programs and strategies used to maintain businesses in technology. Rather than spending all of those years tied up in costly university degrees, it's now a much more logical step for people to learn the skills that they need via a series of short courses focusing on a specific subject, or program, and then joining the workforce within less than one year of completing high school.

The rise in popularity of 'express educational' facilities is also providing a much more affordable option for today's youth, along with the guarantee of a job once they complete their program. This is something that weighs heavily on the minds of university students across the world.

New age schools such as General Assembly and the Holberton School provide the pathway for those students driven to join the workforce at an early age to get the skills that they need, be mentored by experts in the field, and then be placed with some of the top technology companies in the world.

These schools lean heavily on the blended learning style of education as they combine online courses and tutorials with intensive in-class sessions to accelerate the learning process. While these programs aren't for everyone, they are a great pathway for those who are driven and able to commit to some intense study over only a matter of months.

Professional Learning

When it comes to those of us who are already employed and looking to advance our careers, it is only going to become easier and easier to develop new skills and get those promotions and pay rises that we've been chasing.

Similar to the younger generation of job seekers, upskilling and learning how to use new programs and technology has never been easier. Bite-sized learning has made brushing up on new management skills, or learning the new project management process, into a task that you can learn by committing as little as an hour a day to learning.

The average employee in Australia spends approximately one hour each way, every day, traveling to work. Times that by your standard five-day week and over the course of a year you have yourself a solid 500 hours of wasted time in transit.

Now that more and more online courses are available across mobile devices and tablets, this previously wasted travel time no longer has to be spent concentrating your hardest to stay awake while you listen to the excruciatingly painful conversations that take place on public transport.

You can pull out your phone, and instead of skimming through your Facebook and Instagram feed over and over, simply open up your online course and start putting your travel time to work. Ten hours a week is more than enough time to get through most online courses, so over the course of your year - even if you are only working on a course every second week - you will have learned in excess of 20 new skills each year!

The Future of Learning

The evolution of learning with technology is still very much in its infancy. Although things are developing rapidly across the industry, we are only just touching the tip of the iceberg when it comes to what we will soon be able to achieve through online education.

Every week, more and more people are looking online to develop themselves both personally and professionally. And as subject matter experts continue to develop and evolve their content offerings, we can look forward to the quantity and quality of materials evolving at an exponential rate.

So, what should we do from here? Keep taking courses, creating content and helping to get more people involved with the benefits of online learning. Our community is growing, and given that only ten years ago this didn't exist, just imagine where we will be in another ten years from now!

Acknowledgements

There are a few people that I'd like to thank who have assisted in the writing, editing, and publishing of this book.

Firstly, thank you to the founders of GO1 who have been supporting me with writing this book over the past few years. It's been great to have so many amazing minds to bounce ideas off and build out this story.

Thanks to Ricardo Sé Cestari for contributing the chapter titled 'Why Learning is Needed for Innovation.' Ricardo is the Head of People and Culture at GO1.com, and is always ahead of the curve when it comes to understanding workplace trends. Ricardo is also an amazing writer when it comes to conveying these concepts, and his chapter is a great addition to this book.

A huge thank you to my editor Kerrie-Anne Chinn for spending the past year working with me to turn this project into something that hopefully you have really enjoyed reading. Without Kerrie-Anne this project would have taken a lot longer to put together and her writing and editing skills have been a key part of what you are reading as a finished product. Thank you for everything!

I'd also like to thank graphic designer Evan McClellan for creating the cover art and layout for this book, and Ben Gunzburg for the photograph on the back cover. Your creative talent and input is much appreciated, as always.

Finally, thank you to my very understanding partner Tammy Butow, who endured me spending our entire Christmas holiday period in 2016-17 writing the bulk of this book, and who always supports me in everything I do.

Printed in Great Britain
by Amazon